BISHOP ALFRED A. OWENS, JR.

HELP THOU MY UNBELIEF:
and Other Messages of Hope

TS-CQD-080

D1447763

Greater Mt. Calvary Holy Church
Washington, DC

All Scripture quotations are taken from the *Authorized King James Version* of the Bible unless otherwise noted.

Help Thou My Unbelief : and Other Messages of Hope
Copyright © 2003 by Bishop Alfred A. Owens, Jr.
610 Rhode Island Ave., N.E.
Washington, D.C. 20005
Phone: (202) 529-4547

ISBN 1-890146-06-4

Printed in the United States of America

Contents

Foreword

We live in a self-help society, when the shelves of bookstores are filled with "how-to's" that employ New Age strategies for improving life, getting ahead and being a better person. But since the writers of old began penning the Holy Writ, the most accurate and the most comprehensive answers to all of humanity's questions and longings can be found only in the Word of God. While the answers are there and have remained there, all too often life's difficulties and distractions have us looking for answers in all the wrong places, leaving us unsure of where to turn and on whom to call. But according to Romans 10:14,

How then shall they call on him in whom they have not believed? And how shall they believe in him of whom they have not heard? And how shall they hear without a preacher?

It becomes the preacher's task to mine into the Word of God to extract those priceless jewels that give us hope in times of desperation, peace in the time of storm, and direction in the time of confusion.

God uses the "foolishness of preaching" not only to confound the wise, to give wisdom freely to all who ask for it. That is the amazing thing about the Word of God — It's free and It's readily available. But more than just His written Word, God is faithful enough to provide dedicated men and women who will audibly declare the truth of God's Word and to make it applicable to contemporary life and situations. Help My Unbelief is a collection of sermons that will certainly bring the Bible to life in the life of the reader. I encourage you to pour through the riches contained herein, for I am convinced that some of the answers to the questions that have been plaguing your mind are found within these pages.

Evangelist Susie C. Owens, Co-Pastor
Greater Mt. Calvary Holy Church
Washington, DC

1

Help My Unbelief

And one of the multitude answered and said;
Master, I have brought unto thee my son, which
hath a dumb spirit. but if thou canst do any thing,
have compassion on us, and help us. Jesus said unto
him, If thou canst believe, all things are possible to
him that believeth. And straightway the father of the
child cried out, and said with tears, Lord, I believe;
help thou mine unbelief (Mark 9:17-24).

In every one of us, there is a strong, innate
desire to "believe" in something or someone. People
choose to fill this void in various ways. Some take a
holistic or natural approach to life to fill it. Others
choose a spiritual approach to guide them through
life in a quest to not only fill this void but to achieve
peace and success. Regardless of our approach,
there is embedded in each of us a powerful desire to
believe and even hope in something or someone. In
Christendom, we often refer to it as FAITH.

Jesus told his disciples, "Have faith in God
and the faith of God." The Word also warns us that
without faith it is impossible to please Him.
However without further study, we can use these
passages to perpetuate the philosophy that faith and

belief are synonymous. We have been erroneously taught that we need to believe in order to have faith. Yet when we examine them both according to scripture, the two may be connected but not enjoined. Hebrews 11:1,

Faith is the substance of things hoped for,
[BUT] the evidence of things not seen.

When faith and belief stand alone they have a different meaning. Faith leans toward our emotions; it is not based on proof. Belief is the acceptance of truth and reality. Belief leans towards thought or reason. When put together faith and belief mean *the acceptance of something that is true or real.* If we believe something, we accept it to be true. However, unbelief is quite the opposite. Unbelief is *doubt or skepticism.* It suggests maybe or maybe not. Contrary to popular opinion, it is possible to have belief and unbelief at the same time. Our foundation text gives us a good example of this.

In the text, the first thing that grabs our attention is a man, a father who brought his son to Jesus. As a father, a man cannot do anything better for his child than to bring him to Jesus. We see a father introducing his son and his son's situation to Jesus. Before a father introduces his son to sports, before he and his son discuss automobiles and women, the first thing he should do is bring his son to Jesus.

This passage leads us to believe they had a good father and son relationship, because this father brought his son to Jesus seeking a miracle. He did not ignore the situation. He did not abuse or neglect his son because of this situation. He chose to seek help. He chose to seek Jesus! In today's society, a good relationship between a father and son is very rare and usually the father is not the one that will bring his son (s) to Jesus. He leaves it up to the mother. Oh, but what better star in a father's crown than to bring his son (s) to Jesus. Nevertheless, I applaud all the single mothers who are raising sons.

However, I want the single mothers to know that they will never be able to deposit into their son's life what a father can deposit no matter how great the bond is between them. I did not make that up. God just designed it to be that way. I know boys have a bond with their mothers and many have a healthy, close relationship, but there is nothing like a father/son relationship. I believe that is why so many men today are despondent or in trouble. They have missed out on their father/son relationship; therefore; they are seeking relationships in various ways.

As a father, there is nothing better than to make sure sons are taught godly principles that will lead them to Jesus Christ. So many men are dysfunctional because their fathers did not introduce them to Jesus. They have had dads to introduce them to drugs, alcohol, and so forth, but when they introduce their sons to Jesus, it makes a difference. That is one of the reasons why we have so many men who abuse women. They do not respect them. They only see women as sex objects because they have never been taught to value women even as precious stones (Proverbs 31:10-12). They missed out on having a positive relationship with their father who should have lead by example how to revere and nurture women. There are men whose main objective is to get women into bed. Their father did not train them how to love and respect women because either their fathers were doing the same thing or were absent as well in their lives.

I try to get Christian men to mentor young men that are being raised by a single mother because I know the value or positive impact a father figure can have and the negative impact an absentee father can have in their lives. I never knew what it was like to be hugged by my father. I never heard my father say, "Alfred, I love you." I never had my father affirm me and make me feel important. I grew up in the lifestyle of an abusive father. My dad abused alcohol, fought my mother, and cussed us both out. I never knew what it was to have a good relationship with my father. But when I met Jesus, I learned and I know what a father's love is all about. However, it did not replace my natural father.

There is something about a bond that God intended for a natural father to have with his son. There is something only a man in his intended role can give to another man, just like there is something only a woman in her intended role can give to another woman. It is call affirmation-- *establishment, helping you to feel like you are somebody.* That is why so many men mistakenly turn to a homosexual lifestyle because they are looking for a male bond relationship. There are those who will see a boy switching and immediately call him a "sissy" and will believe that he will grow up to be gay. If you search his background, more than likely, you will find a male role model missing in the home. Do not think that I am excusing a homosexual lifestyle; I am not. God can deliver us from anything. However before we call someone gay, we should search the root. A big part of who we are is related to our history.

The same applies to those who act "macho" or like a "thug." This negative lifestyle may have steered them towards a life that robbed people, and now, they are in prison because there was no positive male role model in the family. Men that try to be tough and macho are missing something as well. They are missing the image of a gentle father who desires to see the mother of his children treated with tenderness and respect. For those of us who are married, we know it is hard raising children with parents in the house. That is why I get so upset with "dead beat dads" that have three or four children spread all over town many times by different women. They will not give any financial support and will not see their children or even take the time to tell them "happy birthday." The Bible states in 1 Timothy 5:8,

> *But if any provide not for his own, and especially for those of his own house he hath denied the faith, and is worse than an infidel.*

Men, if your seed has caused that child to be created and birthed into this world, you should take an active role and play an important part in that child's life. You should not have that mother tracking you down and fighting you in and out of court to pay child support. I do not care if you have to work two jobs—part time and full time—you need to own up to your responsibility. No one has a baby by himself or herself. And women, do not deny the father the opportunity to bond with his child (ren). I do not care what you have against your "baby's daddy." You need to encourage him to live up to his responsibility and bond with his child (ren).

I admire this man in our scripture text because he brings his problem son to Jesus. The boy was demon-possessed. The scripture calls it *a dumb spirit.* The spirit had robbed him of his speech. He was given to seizures, fits of rage, and destructive behavior. He would foam at the month, gnash his teeth, roll on the ground, and become stiff as a board (Mark 9:18).

I imagine it was a hard spirit to handle! Have you ever had to handle "hard spirits?" I will answer it for you; some of you had a hard spirit before you came to Jesus. It was hard for you and others to deal with that spirit. Thank God for His saving power, which redeems us.

This father brought his demon-possessed boy to Jesus. However, we learn that before he brought his son to Jesus, he brought him to Jesus' disciples, but they had no power to help. *And I spake to thy disciples that they should cast him out; and they could not* (Mark 9:18).

Every disciple of Christ is put to the test as to whether we will "put up" or "shut up." It is time to possess what we profess! How many have testified on the mountaintop but lived in the valley? The time will come when the "proof will be in the putting." In other words, the time will come when we have to put what we have been talking about into practice or be quiet about our so-called "power with God."

In scripture, we learn through a parable that trees bring forth fruit. Matthew 7:17-20,

> *Even so every good tree bringeth forth good fruit: but a corrupt tree bringeth forth evil fruit. A good tree cannot bring forth evil fruit, neither can a corrupt tree bring forth good fruit. Every tree that bringeth not forth good fruit is hewn down, and cast into the fire. Wherefore by their fruits ye shall know them.*

The gist of the parable is to convey that we are supposed to be the trees that bring forth fruit (i.e., productive and life giving). Regretfully, we have too many trees with no fruit on them. We have too many people "talking the talk," but not "walking the walk." Even with the Holy Ghost living inside of us, some of us could not pray a fly away.

When we use the name of Jesus, we have to have some power behind it. God recognizes the power in that name <u>with</u> a lifestyle that goes with it. Jesus told his disciples that the reason why they could not cast the devil out is because *through prayer and fasting* (Mark 9:29). In essence, He was telling them an encounter with the enemy is no "cake walk." We have to be prepared to do battle and exercise our God-given authority in order to achieve success. Often, this requires a purging or cleansing of all the "junk" we absorb in this world to be able to stand with God in His power to cast the devil out. The devil cannot stand God's glory. When we are cleansed from all hindrances, God can move through us to change the person or situation. To do so, we need to take the appropriate steps to concentrate on God and not what is going on around us. A good way to do so is through fasting and praying (together). They require sacrifice and focus, which foster unparalleled determination. To turn down your plate and give up (for some of us) our favorite pass time—food—requires restraint that is birthed through massive need. That is why I do not believe that a person cannot fast, because if trouble hits hard enough, fasting does not seem that hard. Some say. "I do not know, Bishop. I have a sickness that will not allow me to fast." Well, just keep living, because when trouble knocks on your door and you cannot figure a way out, not only will you willingly fast, but also in many cases you will lose your appetite. Do not tell me you cannot fast. Trouble will bring the best out of you!

Jesus looked at this problem child and said, *how long has he been like this?* The father said, *since he was a child,* (Mark 9:21) suggesting he is at least a teenager. No matter how old our child (ren) are we can still bring them to Jesus. If we cannot bring them physically, we can bring them to God in prayer. My son is 30. I cannot make him come to church, but I can bring him to Jesus in prayer every morning I wake up. Some of us have missed the point of bringing people to Jesus in prayer. We see it as trivial. We might not be able to bring that loved one by the hand to the altar, but we can call his or her name out to the Lord in prayer everyday knowing that,

> *The eyes of the LORD are upon the righteous, and his ears are open unto their cry* (Psalms 34:15).

The boy in the text is so possessed that it almost killed him. The father said, *have compassion, and help us* (Mark 9:22). I believe compassion is often missing in the church. The church has "sympathy" but not compassion. Compassion is s*ympathy* **COMBINED** *with the desire to help.* In other words, sympathy is when we share the feeling of someone else. With compassion, we not only share the feelings of others, but we **DO SOMETHING** to help. I know a lot of people who are quick to verbally express how sorry they are for us or how pitiful they feel towards our situation, but won't do anything to help us get out of our condition. I do not need sympathy. I need some compassion! If I am hungry, do not tell me you are going to pray "my strength in the Lord" because I think I can be stronger in the Lord if I had something to eat!

I researched the word *help* used in this passage just for the purpose of this sermon. In the original language of this context --*help* means, *put an end to this.* Anybody need God to put an end to something? He did not say, "help us" in the generic since of the word help. He said, "help us" meaning put *an end to this --I am tired.* In other words, my son has been like this since he was a baby, and I do not want this to last another day!

9

Jesus almost insults the man who asked for help. He said, *If you can believe, all things are possible.* One thing I like about this father is he cried out with tears in his eyes, *Lord I believe help my unbelief.* In other words, I believe you, but just in case there is something in me that does not want to believe, help that part of me. Have you ever believed God but you needed help? At the same time you believed God, unbelief was also there. Have you ever had those two spirits working in you at the same time? Your heart is saying one thing but your mind is saying another. Your ears are hearing one thing, but your eyes are seeing something else?

We will tell someone else to put a smile on their face and encourage them by saying, "God will bring you out of this, just believe God." We will war and fight, rebuking the devil in that person's life. We will tell him/her, you have the word in you; you have no business looking defeated; let us "touch and agree" for victory. It is different when it is someone else. But when that same situation knocks on YOUR door and comes in uninvited, messing with you on your job or in your family it is not that easy. When it comes to your house, you say, "help my unbelief." It is always easier to believe God for somebody else's marriage, children, or situation than to believe God for yours. When it is personal, we will find unbelief trying to sit beside belief.

The evil spirit refuses to turn his son loose. This father did not want to accept defeat, but it has been so long he did not know what else to do. A good father wants to believe he can always protect his child (ren). He wants to believe he can rectify any injustice or problem--deliverance is possible in the hands of a father. There are times we deal with situations that just when we think we are delivered, just when we think we are free, unbelief rises in our spirit. Some things are easier to believe God for than others. It is different believing God to heal a *headache* than for Him to heal *cancer.*

We believe God based upon what God has already done and what we have seen or heard. But it is very difficult to believe God for anything AND everything. When we make up in our minds to believe God for anything and everything, that is usually when an *unbelief* spirit creeps in. Understand, "talk is cheap." Sure, we will *say* anything, but it is not necessarily true that we *believe* anything. That is why I appreciate the honesty of the man in this text. He believed but it had not happened yet. He was honest with Jesus, help my **doubt**, help my **frustration**, help my **impatience**, help my **anxieties**, help my **confusion**, help my **pain**, and help my **disorder**. In other words, put an end to this! Help me to get rid of this mixture between belief and unbelief.

Just like good and evil is present at the same time so is belief and unbelief; belief is spiritual and unbelief is carnal. There is always opposition between the spiritual and the carnal. Belief must increase and unbelief must decrease. It is a trick of the enemy to let unbelief triumph over belief because that would make God a liar. If we cannot believe He is trust-worthy, we have no hope. The Bible states in Mark 9:23, *Jesus said unto him, If thou canst believe, all things are possible to him that believeth.*

Therefore, it is the enemy's job to plant unbelief in our spirits. The Bible states, *when you pray stand believing* (Mark 11:24).

Have you prayed for someone and it seemed like the situation got worse? I know I have. I almost felt like maybe I should not have prayed at all. It was not that we did not believe. We give tithes and offerings faithfully yet, the car breaks down unexpectedly; the promotion that we thought we were going to get was denied; the job was downsized; there is a sickness in our bodies and the doctor cannot find the problem; and the people we trust and had confidence in deceived us. We read God's word and believe that *weeping may endure for a night, but joy is coming in the morning* (Psalm 30:5), but we say to ourselves, it sure has been nighttime a LONG time. We believe His Word in Psalm 34:19 that, *many are the afflictions of the righteous: but the Lord delivers them out of them all.*

But it seems as though we are overly afflicted. We believe after the rain the sun will shine, but it has not stopped raining yet, and as a matter of fact, now it is pouring!

Once we say we believe, unbelief will flare up to make us feel like a fool. There is nothing worse than "confessing" and holding firmly to a belief to have it not ring true. It is embarrassing and shameful. That is why it often takes so much energy to fight off unbelief.

In the midst of that father's conflict between belief and unbelief, Jesus healed the boy. He put an end to whatever the problem was in his life. The God that we serve can let our situation linger, while giving us grace to handle it OR He can put an end to it! There are three things to remember about unbelief:

Principle number one,

Unbelief does not make faith ineffective.

For what if some did not believe? shall their unbelief make the faith of God without effect? God forbid: yea, let God be true, but every man a liar (Romans 3:3-4).

Principle number two,

Unbelief does not stop God when He gets ready to move.

If God said it, that settles it, whether we believe it or not. All we need to know is did *God say it,* and if He did, that settles it! God is sovereign. God can do whatever He wants to do, however He wants to do it, and whenever He wants to do it. God will move in spite of whatever or whoever is in the way.

Principle number three,

Unbelief does not cancel out God.

Psalm 14:1 states,

> *The fool hath said in his heart, There is no God. They are corrupt, they have done abominable works, there is none that doeth good.*

Scientists doubt Him, but He is still God; Psychologists doubt Him, but He is still God; some of our friends and family members doubt Him, but He is still God. His existence is not nullified by our cynicism.

Somebody needs to proclaim, "Lord, I believe you. I have been dealing with this for so long, help my unbelief." In Mark 9:25, Jesus heals the boy and said, *This will never return again.* Grab a hold of faith and say, "Lord, help my unbelief, put an end to it." By **IT** meaning, whatever our situation may be at the moment. Now, believe that He has put an end to that situation and celebrate!

2

God Wants Us to Know Him

Then Paul stood in the midst of Mars' hill, and said, Ye men of Athens. I perceive that in all things ye are too superstitious. For as I passed by, and beheld your devotions, I found an altar with this inscription, TO THE UNKNOWN GOD. Whom therefore ye ignorantly worship, him declare I unto you (Acts 17:22-23).

It is interesting to look at how society can affect our judgment and alter truth by perverting it with fictitious ideas of spirituality. It becomes "gospel" when it suits their objectives. When challenged, society tries to institute laws or solicit the help of celebrities to justify or add validity to their claims. But, these celebrities are called "idols" for a reason.

Preying on our need for a spiritual connection, society has tricked the weak and uninformed into believing that they hold the keys to happiness and fulfillment. Yet, Jesus said, *I came that you might have life and that more abundantly*

(John 10:10). So how did so many of us get off track? Let us look at our scripture text for reference.

The apostle Paul in his travels goes through Athens. He discovers a group that is very religious. Yet, this very religious group does not know the true and living God. Religion in its formality and tradition cannot replace God. Religion is a system of beliefs and/or worship style that people follow with devotion and seriousness. But, religion does not *guarantee* knowledge of God.

Our society, nation, and even the world are extremely religious. There are Baptists, Methodist, Catholics, Presbyterians, Episcopalians, and Pentecostals who are seriously devoted to their denomination but do not really know God in an intimate and personal way.

Paul told the men of Athens, I have watched you worship God but not in spirit and in truth. Today, there are people who say they are worshipping God but they have the wrong kind of spirit, and they do not know the truth. Quoting scriptures and memorizing verses of the Bible is no sign that we know God. Going to church Sunday after Sunday—morning, noon, and night—is not a sign that we know God. Following the bulletin and "the order of service" does not mean we know God. We can dot every religious "I" and cross every religious "T" and still not know God!

Do we know him? We know all of the moves, but we do not know the MOVER. We know the right songs and we mimic the dances, shouting up and down the church isles, but do we know Him? We move our mouths in praise—lifting our hands and raising our voices—yet some of us do not know God.

Paul wanted them to know they were ignorantly worshipping Him out of their religious traditions and out of superstition. I want to make it very clear right now **superstition** and God do not go hand-in-hand; **luck** and God do not go together; the **horoscope** and God do not go together; the **ouija board** and God do not go together; **fortune telling** and God do not go together; **black magic**, black cats, a rabbit's foot, a horseshoe, a chain around an ankle, or a red bag in our pocketbook do not go together with God. Any form of **witchcraft** and God do not go together. These are all things that falsely represent a higher power and sense of security that we believe will help us or help God help us.

God is God all by Himself. He does not need the lottery to bless us. He does not need bat dust or black magic to bless us. God does not need any graven images or statues to guard over us or help prosper us. God does not need any rosary or beads in our pocketbook to aid in His ability to forgive us. He does not need us to burn any candles or incense or lay down any roots to get His attention. God does not need a crystal ball to know our future or a séance to aid resurrecting the dead. All these things mimic the truth and lie to us. They bring Him no glory. Therefore, if it is not glorifying God, we better leave it alone.

With this group, Paul was dealing with a *form of godliness*. The Word of God lets us know that in the last days, many will come in the name of

Christ and will try to deceive the very elect. Matthew 24:24 states,

> *For there shall arise false Christs; and false prophets, and shall shew great signs and wonder; insomuch that, if it were possible, they shall deceive the very elect.*

Confucianism, Buddhism, and that little piece of paper we get out of a fortune cookie will not lead us to knowing God. Why? Those things are man-made answers to a spiritual connection with God. We would not need a "form of godliness" if we simply knew GOD. But that would require we follow His word whole-heartily without adding our "two-cents."

I love the movie, *What's Love Got to Do With It*. I have seen that movie at least three or four times. It is an autobiographical movie that depicts the life (the good and the bad) of Tina Turner. It shows how she met her husband, Ike Turner, and chronicles their abusive marriage. I think the movie showed brilliant acting by Angela Basset who played Tina Turner. In my opinion, she should have won an Academy Award for her performance. In the movie, Tina Turner turns to Buddhism and practices meditation to find relief from her tumultuous relationship with her husband. I read in an article that after the movie many people turned to meditation following her example and this bothered me. Please understand that if our worship does not point us to the one and true God we better leave it alone! We use to sing a song years ago, "If you ever need the Lord before, you sure do need him now." I think that song is more appropriate in this 21st

Century than times past. This is the time to know God. He is the peace giver and our only true hope. All we need to do is MEDITATE on Him (Isaiah 26:3).

Paul said, "I looked on your altar and written on your altar is the inscription, TO THE UNKNOWN GOD.*" I find it interesting that even in their ignorance they knew through their spirit-man they were created to worship. They just did not KNOW God for who He is. Believe me. It is not enough to join the church, join the usher board, sing in the choir, or unite with an auxiliary or ministry. It is not enough to graduate from a Bible institute or pay tithes, and still not know God in a personal way. Some believe good works through these different things will bring them salvation. But if the Lord Jesus Christ is not written on the tables of our hearts, all our *works* will not mean a thing. The Church must come together and declare, "We need to know God." Do you know what is on the altar of your heart?

The altar is the place of sacrifice. Matthew 6:21 states,

> *For where your treasure is, there will your heart be also.*

Is money written on your altar? Is prosperity symbolized by cars, land, and houses written on your altar? Is lust written on your altar? What is your passion? Whatever it is, you must recognize that —

> *no man can serve two masters. He will love one and hate the other* (Matthew 6:24).

Therefore, you have to make a choice as to whom you will serve.

Everything that we are seeking will fall into place if we seek <u>first</u> the Kingdom of God, and allow Jesus to be Lord of our lives. It is recorded in Matthew 6:33,

> *But seek ye first the kingdom of God, and his righteousness, and all these things shall be added unto you.*

Is Jesus on your altar? He should be much more than an associate or a casual friend. He MUST BE more than a one-night stand or to relieve tension when we mess up and get in trouble. We should not seek Him when it is *convenient*. He should be our God at all times – good and bad.

There are three fundamental things I believe to knowing God.

I. We must know God for ourselves and not through somebody else.

Yes, I am glad "somebody prayed for me," but there comes a time when we have to learn how to pray for ourselves. I recognize somebody prayed for me, which helped me get where I am today, but I also had to learn how to communicate and talk to God for myself. Second-hand knowledge is not good enough! We need our own testimony just as the writer mentioned in this song:

> *I came to Jesus just as I was—weary, worn, and sad. But, I found in Him a resting-place and He has made me glad.*

We need to PERSONALLY know that "can't nobody do us like Jesus." People can point us in the right direction and show us the way. Thank God for them. But as the old cliché goes, "you can lead a horse to water but you cannot make him drink." Thank God for pastors and leaders who lead us, but we must ultimately know God for ourselves.

II.   Head knowledge is good, but heart knowledge is better.

Our intellect is not enough to see us through in life. Some of the most brilliant men and women are also some of the most miserable and depressed. Paul was ultimately saying to the people of Athens, you are real serious BUT seriously wrong. Make no mistake about it. They were an intelligent group. They were very astute. Yes, they had a lot of wisdom and knowledge, but Paul wanted them to know wisdom and knowledge did not mean anything if they did not know God! We might be highly educated, but if we do not have salvation, we are just EDUCATED FOOLS!

Teachers of philosophy and Greek have taught me. Some specialized in Plato, Sartre, and Aristotle, but it is not enough in this life to receive carnal knowledge. Likewise, sermons, spiritual workshops, retreats, and conferences do not mean anything if we do not know God in our hearts. David wrote in Psalms 119:11,

Thy word have I hid in mine heart, that I might not sin against thee.

Some of us have the Word (i.e., the Holy Bible) hidden in our homes—we have one in our living room, dining room, bathroom, and bedroom. But, David did not say he hid the Word in his HOME. That is the wrong "H." Some of us carry the Word in our hand faithfully and some of the Bibles that we carry are just as big as we are. But, it is not enough to have it in HAND. That too, is the wrong "H." Then, some of us have the Word in our HEAD, so much so that some might think we are a walking Biblical encyclopedia! I had an uncle named, Uncle Bud. Every time Uncle Bud would drink too much alcohol, he would start quoting scriptures. He would love it when I would come around because I was the preacher in the family and he knew at that time he knew more scriptures than I did. But Uncle Bud had it in his head. That is the wrong "H" also. We might have more "degrees" than a thermometer, but I do not care if you studied at Howard, Yale, or Princeton University, or if you received your degree in the mail, if you do not know GOD, you do not know anything! You have to have Him in your heart. I am reminded of an old, old song:

> *It's in my heart this melody of love divine. It's in my heart that I am His and he is mine. It's in my heart, how can I help but sing and shout. It's in my heart, it's in my heart. Some folks sing to pass the weary night along. Some folks sing just to entertain a worldly song. But I sing because I worship God in song. It's in my heart, it's in my heart. [Personal*

interjection] Some folks sing because they have a pretty voice. Some folks sing because they need the money and they haven't got no other choice. But I sing because I love to rejoice. It's in my heart, it's in my heart. You ask me how I know that God is real. You want to know how my savior makes me feel. You ask me why I love to do His will. It's in my heart, it's in my heart [end of interjection]. You ask how I find the time to fast and pray. You want to know how I can smile when things are far from gay. You ask me how I can sing His praises come what may. It's in my heart, it's in my heart. When death shall come and carried me away. When my voice is hush and I'm sleeping beneath the cold, cold clay. I'll rise again and oh what a glorious day. It's in my heart, it's in my heart.

We do not need more information, but SALVATION; we do not need more information, but REVELATION; we do not need more information, but TRANFORMATION; we do not need more information, but DEDICATION; we do not need more information, but CONSECRATION; we do not need more information, but INSPIRATION. AND, we need to have IT IN OUR HEARTS.

III.   *We cannot know God through emotions and feelings.*

It does not matter how we *feel*, God is still worthy to be praised! If the truth be told, some days we feel like praising God and some days we do not. From day-to-day, we do not always feel the same. That is why we cannot operate based on our emotions. How much we shout and dance in church is no indicator that we know God. I wonder sometimes if these "dances" are really holy anyway because some of us can really get down! Commonly, music will excite most African Americans. Some of the "most saved," including myself will find ourselves (unknowingly, of course) patting our feet to a different beat other than gospel music and then catch ourselves and realize the type of music we are listening to is not our type of music. Now, I know some of us cannot *identify* with that because we do not catch ourselves—we will just flow with it and get down! What I want you to know is our emotions will play tricks on us, so we cannot place our knowledge of God in emotionalism.

   A lot of people have zeal. They will take off running all around the church, jumping up and down so much that the nurses in the church congregation will have to hold them down. The nurses in my church have been trained not to let them get too wild. They know that if we get too wild it is not the Holy Ghost moving through us but rather our flesh craving attention. They know the

Holy Ghost will not let us hurt anyone else or ourselves. Anytime we need five or six people to hold us down, that is not the Holy Spirit but a violent spirit! If you want to dance, go ahead and do your little dance AND sit down! If you are "slain in the Spirit" just go ahead and lay down gently instead of wildly kicking your legs and feet.

I had one of the nurses in my church tell me that there was a person who supposedly was in the Spirit that was dancing and acting very wild. When some of the nurses tried to hold the person to keep him from hurting himself and others around him, the person became livid and said in an angry voice, "Turn me loose. Didn't you hear me? I said do not touch me." Now, this person was supposed to be in the Spirit. Yet, they had the presence of mind to get angry with another saint of the church. What I am trying to convey is it does not matter how high we jump, how loud we holler, or how often we speak in tongues. That is not a true indication that we know God or have a right relationship with Him. I have heard many people say, "HALLELUJAH" in church, and in the parking lot leaving church, curse somebody out. People will come to church, sing praise and worship songs to God, and then turn around and say, "I'll smack the hell out of you if you bother me." I will not criticize you if you do not dance or shout. All I want is for you to have a right relationship with God. I realize there are some people who will not dance or shout but will internalize the blessing.

Since God has always been concerned that we know Him, what is a clear indication or sign for us? If it is not through someone else, through our intellect, or emotions, how do we know Him?

To *KNOW* is *to perceive or understand as a fact or truth*.
To *KNOW* is *to apprehend clearly or with certainty*.
To *KNOW* is *to have something established or fixed in our minds*.
To *KNOW* is *to comprehend through experience or practice*.

How do we know if we really know Him? Do we just know? NO! The Bible states in I John 2:3-4,

> *And hereby we do know that we know him, if we keep his commandments. He that saith, I know him, and keepeth not his commandments, is a liar, and the truth is not in him.*

Whatever He commanded us to do we can do it. I John 5:3 states,

> *For this is the love of God, that we keep his commandments: and his commandments are not grievous.*

His commandments were not given to trouble or grieve us. He has not told us to do anything that is not in our power to do. Let me reiterate it again, His commandments are not grievous! Titus 1:16 states,

> *They profess that they know god; but in works they deny him, being abominable, and disobedient, and unto every good work reprobate.*

Do not just "talk-the-talk" but "walk-the-walk." 2 Timothy 1:12 states,

> *For which cause I also suffer these things: nevertheless I am not ashamed: for I know whom I have believed, and am persuaded that he is able to keep that which I have committed unto him against that day.*

Our lifestyles will prove if we know God. God cannot keep anyone or anything unless it is committed to Him. We cannot commit to somebody we do not know. This is a message that should make us examine ourselves, because in the troubling days ahead, we will have to know God for ourselves to find peace and hope. He is our refuge in times of trouble. No matter what lies ahead, He is our help. More than anything, God wants us to know Him. Now, the question remains do you know Him?

In Matthew 7:22-23, Jesus warns us,

> *Many will say to me in that day, Lord, Lord, have we not prophesied in thy name? and in thy name have cast out devils? and in thy name done many wonderful works? And then will I profess unto them, I never knew you: depart from me, ye that work iniquity.*

3

A Beautiful Mind

Have this mind among yourselves, which is yours in Christ Jesus (Philippians 2:5).

In a world of "high fashion," there is an enormous emphasis placed on achieving and maintaining beauty. "Beautiful people" are in many ways favored. They are looked upon as the epitome of achievement or viewed as gifted and showered with love. Those who are <u>not</u> considered physically beautiful are often shunned or belittled. Even our children taunt and tease each other because of the way they look. However, a beautiful mind is more important than a beautiful body. I have seen many beautiful bodies with ugly, messed up minds. We put so much effort in beautifying our bodies in hopes of being liked and adored. It is not enough to have ears pierced. Now, people have nose and navel piercing. I am not sure if God intended for us to put all those holes in our bodies. I am not sure if God intended for us to place tattoos everywhere to make statements or "accent" our skin. We put so much emphasis on beautifying the body that people do not know when or where to draw the line. Do not misunderstand me. Beauty has its place, but we neglect the maintenance of our minds. We spend precious time, money, and energy trying to beautify the physical part of the body, but we leave the mental part of our being untouched.

There are mental hospitals all over the country that help the unbalanced. Some of us have come across a few people who were not hospitalized for mental issues, but needed to be admitted. Some of us have been around people that are twisted and messed up in their minds, looking good on the outside but disturbed. Regretfully, it does not come to light until we have known them long enough because we judge them outwardly before looking inwardly. Once we do, we realize they do not have a beautiful mind.

The mind is *the element, part, substance, or process of our being that reasons*. The mind thinks, feels, wills, perceives, and judges. The mind is the totality of the conscience and unconscious mental processes or activities. The mind has to do with our intellect and our understanding. It is true; the mind is a "terrible thing to waste." I have met some people who have wasted their minds on drugs, alcohol, riotous living and sexual promiscuity. It has diminished their appeal.

Nobody is born with a beautiful mind. I do not care how pretty that baby looks. Nobody is born with a beautiful mind because of the sin of Adam and Eve in the Garden of Eden. They disobeyed God and ate from the Tree of the Knowledge of Good and Evil, effecting every generation to follow. Withstanding, we were born in sin. Thus, we came out of our mother's womb with a carnal mind. It is called the Adamic nature. It is named after Adam whose disobedience to God conceived an ungodly mind that needed to be transformed.

We cannot begin to develop a beautiful mind until we are Born Again. Through the saving power of the death, burial, and resurrection of Jesus Christ, we can earnestly say, He is Lord. The apostle Paul says to the church of Philippi, *Let this mind be in you, which was also in Christ Jesus*. In other words, let the mind of Jesus, which is a beautiful mind, become our mind so we can win the battle of our carnal minds.

Truly, there is a war going on and the casualties are our minds. That is why confusion often sets in because God wants our minds, but at the same time, the devil wants them too. That is why it is so hard to do the right thing all the time. The more we try the more we fail because our minds cannot comprehend that there is a spiritual war going on causing havoc. God is on one side and the devil is on the other. Paul described this "tug-of-war" like this,

> *When I would do good [when it is in my mind], evil is always present* (Romans 7:21).

The devil is determined to make sure we do not have beautiful minds. The enemy wants us to have a confused mind, double mind, depressed mind, oppressed mind, stressed mind, and suppressed mind! He would rather we have a mind that is conformed and shaped by the world, because he knows if God ever gets a hold of us, we will be transformed *by the renewing of the mind*. The mind is made beautiful by the power of God. Is there anybody who used to have a messed up, low down, dirty, mind but God snatched you and touched your mind and now you have a beautiful mind?

There are three characteristics of a beautiful mind. The first is,

A changed mind, different from how it used to operate.

In other words, salvation says, I have changed my mind. It comes down to making a decision to allow our minds to be regulated by the Holy Ghost. In order to do so, we must first receive salvation.

If we want to define salvation and its basics, it is transformation by the renewing of our minds. If we want to know why some people we know do not do drugs anymore, they have changed their minds. God bless the 12-steps program, Alcoholics Anonymous (AA), and all the other programs. But still, we are delivered today because we changed our minds. If we tell the truth, those of us Born Again tried programs, we were in and out of ministries, and kept going back and forth with the very thing we were struggling with UNTIL we told ourselves, this is not going to work for me anymore. Then, we changed our minds. Now people can dangle that thing that had our minds consumed and bound with in our faces, but we will walk right over it or through it.

A carnal mind is not a beautiful mind; it is enmity against God. The Word of God states,

> *For to be carnally minded is death but to
> be spiritually minded is life and peace*
> (Romans 8:6).

The changed mind has a before and after. The mind
that changed has a past and present. If we cannot
celebrate a "before and after," "then and now," or
"was and is," we do not have a changed mind,
because at some point, there is an obvious
transformation. The Bible states in Isaiah 26:3,

> *Thou wilt keep him in perfect peace, whose
> mind is stayed on thee: because he trusteth
> in thee.*

We might feel like it at times, but real saints do not
have nervous breakdowns—we have breakthroughs.
God will help us as we make the change. God
knows when we are just "shucking and jiving"
about making a change. But when we are sincere
with God, He said,

> *There hath no temptation taken you but
> such as is common to man: but God is
> faithful, who will not suffer you to be
> tempted above that ye are able; but will
> with the temptation also make a way to
> escape, that ye may be able to bear it*
> (1Corinthians 10:13).

The change is basically an attitude change.
We need to begin to change our minds about *life*,
liberty, and *the pursuit of happiness*. What we
thought was **life** was really killing us. But when we
changed our minds, we found out that He is the only
one that can give life. We need to begin to change
our minds about **liberty** because what we thought
was making us free was really binding us. The more

liquor we drank, the more cocaine we snorted, the more women or men we were sexually involved with was not making us free. But we found freedom and liberty in Christ—

If the Son therefore shall make you free, ye shall be free indeed (John 8:36).

We need to begin to change our minds about the **pursuit of happiness**. What we thought was happiness was sadness. Why? Because God was not in it, and anything God is not in we cannot really enjoy. When we find God and we change our minds, He satisfies us! He will satisfy us without drugs, liquor, women, or men. Are these things still around? Yes, but they do not have an effect on us when we have a changed mind! Next,

---

A beautiful mind is a rearranged mind.

There is a different ORDER to our thinking. When we rearrange something, we position it and move it. The things that use to be priority to us have been rearranged. What is important now was not important before we received a rearranged mind. Things that use to feel like a heavy weight upon us do not matter now. We have re-prioritized and rearranged the order of our thinking. God has allowed it so that the essential things and the nonessential things *do not* compete with each other. Consequently, we know what is important and what is not important. There is a difference in the way we handle things. There was a time when we would curse somebody out without thinking about it. There was a time we sought retribution for every little thing done wrong to us. There was a time we lived for vengeance, and we were ready at all times for a fight. But now when people try to harm us, God has rearranged our minds to such a place where we can earnestly request, "Father forgive them for they do not know that I am a child of the Most High." Know, God can handle people better than we can so let God handle it!

A rearranged mind has been properly adjusted. Yes, it *was* the club to go to every weekend, but now the church. It *was* the party to dance at, but now it is the prayer meeting. It *was* luck we believed in, but now it is favor. It *was* fate that we counted on, but now it is faith. It *was* chance that dictated our lives, but now it is choice. It *was* the lottery and casinos that we put stock in, but now it is tithes and offerings, and the Lord *loves a cheerful giver.* It *was* happy hour that made our day, but now *THIS IS THE DAY the Lord has made. I will REJOICE and be GLAD in it,* regardless of the day I am having! Take time to give God praise if you have moved from an "hour" to a "day." Have you had your mind rearranged? Philippians 4:8 states,

> *Whatsoever things are true, whatsoever things are honest, whatsoever things are just, whatsoever things are pure, whatsoever things are lovely, whatsoever things are of good report; if there be any virtue, and if there be any praise think on these things.*

There is a song that we sing:

I woke up this morning with my mind stayed on Jesus and when I rose this morning, I didn't have no doubt. I knew the Lord would take care of me.

I thank God for a beautiful mind. Thirdly,

A beautiful mind is no longer an estranged mind.

We were estranged, separated, and disconnected from God, but with a changed mind, He is as close to us as the air we breathe. The Bible states,

He is a very present help in the time of trouble (Psalms 46:1).

God use to be so distant from us because we lived so far from Him. We were like the prodigal son—fallen away from God, estranged, and mentally disconnected by choice. Sin alienated us from God. Sin removed us from the original intent and plan that God had for our lives. The enemy brought estrangement and separated us from God. In times past, God did not leave me; I left Him. I distanced myself from God because of sin. I put people, places, ambition, and finances between God and me, but "Lord, I am coming home." No more estrangement. Those things that separated me from God I told them GOODBYE. Even as the prodigal son, I am coming home where love is waiting for me.

That is my appeal to you dear reader. If you are one of those who needs to come home, and if there is a gulf that is between you and God because

of bad choices, it is time to receive the mind of Christ. You cannot have a beautiful mind being so far away. I am not worried about your body, because if you give God your mind, your body will follow! Trust, obey, and believe on Him
and He will make you beautiful—mind, body, and soul. CHANGED, REARRANGED, and no longer ESTRANGED!

4

Deliverance

*He that dwelleth in the secret place of the most
High shall abide under the shadow of the Almighty.
I will say of the LORD, He is my refuge and my
fortress: my God; in him will I trust. Surely he shall
deliver thee from the snare of the fowler, and from
the noisome pestilence (Psalms 91:1-3).*

Traps by our adversary, Satan, are set for us
everyday. Some call them "temptations." Others
refer to them as "trials." No matter which form they
take shape in, these traps are meant to destroy us.
They may destroy our innocence, integrity, desire,
dreams, or will. We can become so entangled in
these "snares" that achieving our destiny in God is
jeopardized. How does it come to this? What can
be done about it?

We throw out words like addicted, genetic
flaw, or phobia to make excuses for our behavior.
But when we peel back the layers of our despair and
become transparent, we see that what we really
need is deliverance. Sometimes it is deliverance
from the enemy. Other times it is simply
deliverance from ourselves. In order to achieve it,
we must reach up and out to God for divine
intervention. We have to let go of our will and our

independence and put total faith in God, knowing He can bring us out. We can achieve victory in Christ if we put our trust in Him.

Psalms 91 is a confession of the writer's, [David], complete confidence in God. He expresses his personal trust in the Lord. He gives a personal testimony–My God is the one I can trust when I cannot trust anybody else. He gives us the formula for deliverance by saying those of us who live close to God and get into His presence have the assurance that they are protected and need not fear evil. Like David elegantly wrote in Psalms 23,

> *Though I walk through the valley of the shadow of death I will fear no evil for thou art with me.*

We have an assurance that God protects us. That means we are protected against human enemies, persecution and demonic forces and spirits. Even though enemies rise up, persecution comes, demonic forces and spirits try to invade our territory, they will not overtake us. They will try and invade our lives, but they will not succeed. I have had some depressing times in my life, and I faced some frustrating and anxious moments, but I am so glad I have not faced anything yet that has taken me out. That is a blessing right there! That "thing" came to take me out, but by God's grace, it did not. It was designed, planned, and set-up for my defeat; it was supposed to tear me asunder, but what the devil meant for evil, God reversed it for my good! Right NOW it is working for my good. It is recorded in Isaiah 54:17,

No weapon that is formed against thee shall prosper; and every tongue that shall rise against thee in judgment thou shalt condemn. This is the heritage of the servants of the LORD. And their righteousness is of me, saith the LORD.

No weapon that is formed against us shall succeed. It was formed, and we even saw it right up in our faces, but it did not work! Thank God it did not take us out. HALLEJUAH! It came to me, but it could not stay. All of us who tried liquor and did not become an alcoholic, all of us who may have tried marijuana or cocaine but did not get addicted, all of us who may have had several different sexual partners and yet did not contract HIV/AIDS, we better rejoice with a grateful heart! Oh, the devil thought he had us, but we got away. Thank God for mercy. The automobile accident did not kill us. The house caught on fire, but we got out just in time. The pregnancy test should have come out positive but it turned out to be negative. How much praise should we give God for helping us get away?

God is our refuge. God is our fortress. God is our security. We quote the scripture that states,

Surely goodness and mercy shall follow me all the days of my life (Psalms 23:6).

I do not want to cancel out that "surely," but there is another **surely** I want to emphasize. The Bible states in Psalms 91:3,

SURELY [meaning positively, certainly, without a doubt] *He shall deliver me from the snare of the fowler and from the nosience pestilence.*

Deliverance is at hand.

What is the snare of the fowler? The Psalmist uses the image of a trapped bird. *Traps*— things that make us uncomfortable to disturb us, symbolic descriptions of danger. My momma use to pray, "Lord, I thank you for keeping us from danger seen and unseen." In other words, the writer of this passage is referring to anything that might come to *helpless* people, a people that cannot help themselves. My Father is a deliverer from the *snare of the fowler*. The trap set for us won't work!

We have assurance of deliverance from the trap AND the fowler. A fowler is a person who hunts birds. The fowler uses bait, lure, or a snare to subdue his prey. Anyway he can entrap a bird the fowler will do it. Whenever we see "fowler" used in the Bible, it suggests danger! A snare in this case is a slipknot cord or wire pulled tight to wrap and hold tight the legs of the bird after it steps into the loop to get the bait or stumbles into it by accident. The bird is trapped in the snare, either because he is attracted to the bait or he is looped in by accident. I do not know what your case may be, but every one of us at some point has been snared. Many of us were "baited" into the trap because it looked so good! We knew it was a trap, but we took our chances just like a gambler. Some of us are Atlantic City gamblers, Las Vegas gamblers, and Lottery gamblers. Some of us have gambled with our bodies. We say, I am going to take a chance because that looks so good. So, the bait attracted us! Then, some are looped in by accident. They were at the wrong place at the wrong time and accidentally fell into the trap. Some of us did not intend to get into anything. It just happened to be initiated by environmental influences, which led us to believe we needed to be a part of the crowd.

The enemy of our souls is the hunter or fowler. He is consistently and constantly trying to ensnare or trap us. However, the word of God comes with an assurance that those who live close to God shall SURELY be delivered from the snare. To me that means there is no excuse for falling into every trap. There is no excuse for bumping into every obstacle. Our relationship with Christ should help us advert some of these traps. Jesus said in Luke 22:31,

> *And the Lord said, Simon, Simon, behold,*
> *Satan hath desired to have you, that he*
> *may sift you as wheat.*

In other words, Satan wants to destroy you and make nothing out of you. Satan desires to have us and sift us as wheat too. His trap did not stop Peter, and it should not stop us! If Satan can get us back on his turf—just one more time—he will tear us apart. He is waiting for an opportunity to get us back for all the times we said, "Thank you, Jesus." Well, the devil is a liar!

Jesus said, "Satan has desires to sift you as wheat, *but I have prayed for you."* If we look in the Scriptures, we will notice that Peter did mess up. (Matthew 26:31-34, 69-75). But I believe after that incident, Peter got his act together. There might have been other trials and temptations, but I believe he learned with every encounter how to look for the

43

signs of the enemy at work. Through all our "mess-ups," the Lord has been merciful to us. Jesus said,

But I have prayed for thee, that thy faith fail not: and when thou art converted, strengthen thy brethren (Luke 22:32).

From His example, it is imperative that we pray for one another. Like Jesus, we need to cover each other in prayer that we might overcome, and if necessary, survive every snare of the enemy. Intercessors in the Body of Christ are essential. Oh, we did not make it this far on our own. Somebody called out our names in prayer. I am so glad somebody prayed for me!

There are four things that we need to take from Psalms 91 as lessons learned. First,

---

Birds do not know where the fowler has set the snare.

We do not know where the enemy's next move is laid out. Therefore, we have to do more than sit by the wayside and pray. We have to open our big eyes and WATCH, because the enemy is counting on us letting our guard down. The enemy wants to get us off guard and he does that many times through various distractions from cares of this life. We do not know where his next trap is situated so it pays to be alert, looking everywhere for his snares.

Peter admonished us to,

Be sober, be vigilant, be watchful, because your adversary, the devil is like a roaring lion seeking who he may devour (1Peter 5:8).

Be watchful because sometimes he comes as an "angel of light" (2 Corinthians 11:14). The Bible states,

> *If it be possible, in the last days the devil will deceive the very elect* (Matthew 24:24).

That means those who God has called out and set apart. If possible, the enemy will mess with them in hopes of destroying them and anyone associated with them. Why? Because, the fowler capitalizes on SURPRISES. In order for the enemy to be successful, he must deceive us. Therefore, he depends on deceit to be successful. Throughout the New Testament, Jesus kept saying, *be not deceived* and *do not be fooled* (Matthew 24:4; Mark 13:5; Luke 21:8). Secondly,

---

The snare is always disguised or camouflaged.

The hunter makes the trap so the prey does not readily discover it. When the bird is trapped, it is sudden. It leaves the bird astonished and more than likely dead. Likewise, the disguise orchestrated by Satan catches us unaware and before we know it, we are enmeshed. While we are struggling in the trap to get free, we get deeper and deeper entangled. The trap is designed so intricately that we will not get free without a fight. He has designed his trap to be so enticing that we are engulfed before we know what hit us. He has camouflaged it to look like something we cannot live without. He has disguised it to look irresistible. That is why I often quote that old saying, "everything that glitters IS NOT gold" and "the grass always looks greener on the other side." BUT, "if we play with fire (sooner or later), we will get burned."

The disguise goes as far as false doctrine. It is surprising the number of people calling on Jesus and using His name that do not even know Him. That is why the apostle John said, *Try the spirit* (1 John 4:1). In other words, do not assume that what is said or how it is presented is the Truth. John the Beloved said, *See if they be of God.* We get in prayer lines for power and anointing, but what we need to ask God for is *discernment*. Do not be confused. Discernment is not fortune telling. It is when God allows us to see immediately that someone does not mean us any good. I have had people smile in my face and God allowed me to see the frown in their heart. I have had people to give me a hug, and at the same time, I knew they could not stand me. They did not realize I knew their real intentions and feelings. Some of us get fooled because we do not have any discernment. Pray for discernment! If we have it, we cannot be fooled with discernment. That "stuff" that use to fool us cannot fool us anymore. We can look right through the DISGUISE. I do not care how "holy" it looks. If it is not right, God will register it in our spirits. Thirdly,

---

The fowler never puts the snare in the same place.

When we really get delivered from something, the devil does not bother us with that anymore; he fabricates new stuff. He knows that "thing" that had us bound is out of our system. For example, those of us who use to drink would not take money now to take a sip. It turns us completely off. So, he does not set a trap for us with alcohol. He has something else planned. The snare is never put in the same place because (sooner or later) the fowler recognizes that we have wised-up. If we see our "bird buddy" get caught up in that snare, we would be stupid to follow as well. Why? Because, we have seen what it did to us and is doing to our friend. Therefore, we have to be wise and know not to go back to that same place. We have to be wise and cunning enough to go to another place or another level. Yet, with every new level comes a new devil.

Satan is sinister so we have to be two steps ahead of him at all times. If we are not careful, we will "happen upon" the place that he has set up for us. But, the surest way to keep the devil out of our faces is to get in a place with God. The Psalmist David encourages us in our opening Scriptures, *Go into the secret place of the most high.* It does not matter where the trap is set. God through the Holy Ghost becomes our eyes and ears. Then we move to another place—a higher place in God. Then, we won't get entangled again with the yoke of bondage. When we get in the right place, the enemy will flee. The final point is:

The fowler never stops hunting or gives up.

He may go off for a "season." Why? It is not HUNTING SEASON. Anyone that goes hunting knows that hunting season is not all year round. But, he's coming back! Every now and then, we will find ourselves in a place of tranquility, a wonderful period of *stress-free* living. At least, there should be some point in our lives that we can point to what felt like RELIEF. But if something is always bothering us, we have another problem. If we never have any peace then something is definitely wrong. That is a mental problem—a pessimistic spirit. I stay away from people like that. Have you ever met a person that was so pessimistic that nothing is ever right? They are <u>always</u> complaining. When we serve God, there comes a peaceful period where we can take a little breather from the war. Now, it may not last long, but we better grab it and take advantage of it while it is there. We can take a little breather in our spirits, but we cannot relax! That should be the time when we pray as never before.

Normally, we start to pray when we get in the trap. Psalms 23 states,

Lead me not into temptation.

But while everything is calm, easy, and nobody is bothering us, that is the time to pray! Wondering why? When we get into the snare, we will not be able to pray as we should because we are many times overwhelmed and disconnected from God. Yes, there comes a period when it seems like all Hell has broken loose in our lives. However, there also comes a period when God gives us peace. When we are calm in our spirits that is the time to really pray because "hunting season" is getting ready to start up again.

What is the devil doing "off-season?" He is plotting and planning his next move. He has not given up hunting because he knows that in a few days/weeks/months/years that season will start again. He will be out for the kill. John 10:10,

The thief cometh not, but for to steal, and to kill, and to destroy...

In our spiritual life, just like our natural one, the enemy never relaxes. It may seem like he has "lightened up," but he is just getting ready to introduce something more powerful to ensnare us. He never gives up.

Nevertheless, there is a comforting word. The devil is the enemy of the soul BUT God is the keeper of the soul. So, there is a constant war between the enemy and the Keeper. What prompts the writer in Psalms 91 to write,

Surely [no doubt about it] God shall deliver us from the snare or entrapment of the fowler?

It is found in verse 11,

For he shall give his angels charge over thee, to keep thee in all thy ways.

In addition to talking about the snare of the fowler, the writer mentions the noisome pestilence. Noisome meaning, *whatever gets on our nerves.* I equate it with the frustrating buzzing of bees around our heads or the fly that comes in the house and swarms around the dinner table while we are eating. David wrote, *He* [God] *will deliver us from the noisome pestilence.* He might let the situation stay the same, but He will place us so far above the situation that it won't even matter. God <u>may not</u> change the situation or circumstance right away, but He will change us so we can handle it. Those things that use to get on our nerves, we can now ignore. He will deliver us from the harmful, nerve-racking, injurious diseases. He will put His angels in charge of us to guarantee our safety and to keep us in all His ways. Understand, we are not keeping ourselves. There have been angels assigned to our lives. Know that God will deliver us from the snare of the fowler and the noisome pestilence. He does it by putting His angels around us, and they will keep us from harm.

No matter what comes our way, we do not have to be afraid! For every trap the enemy has set, God has made a way of escape. Deliverance is SURELY ours because we have the victory through the Almighty.

5

The Mind of Jesus: What Would Jesus Do?

Let this mind be in you, which was also in Christ Jesus: Who, being in the form of God, thought it not robbery to be equal with God: But made himself of no reputation, and took upon him the form of a servant, and was made in the likeness of men: And being found in fashion as a man, he humbled himself, and became obedient unto death, even the death of the cross (Philippians 2:5-8).

Man's vanity has led him to believe that "self-improvement" absent of the power of the Holy Ghost is obtainable. Yes, we can make strides to better ourselves, and we should do so on a daily basis. But, it is clearly evident throughout society that there are times in our lives that we cannot make a transition from destructive behavior or unwanted habits without Christ.

We teach tiers of success through programs and self-help books. While some of them are very beneficial for dealing with issues in our lives, there is no substitute for the keeping power of the Holy Ghost. Rather than admit it, we offer excuses for unstained success—"old habits are hard to break." If that is the case, it solidifies my point that self-improvement will only take us so far.

A transformation into a *consistently* victorious person starts with a changed mind. We may change clothes, hairstyles, addresses, telephone numbers, and jobs, but until we have a mind change success is only superficial and more than likely temporary. We can get involved with programs to help us through our additive habits and repeat the program over and over again, but none of the rules will apply to our lives until our mind changes.

Those of us who were wrapped-up and tied-up in sin, and did everything we were "big and bad" enough to do, without any remorse or desire to alter our behavior until our minds changed. We can give up and get rid of anything if we change our minds by the renewing power from the Holy Ghost. The only reason why some of us are still dealing with the same thing (s) yearly is we have not changed our minds. Nothing is going to drop out of the sky. There is no magical way to change. Change comes when we decide to change our minds by allowing Jesus Christ to become Lord of our lives!

In our foundation text, the apostle Paul is trying to convince the church of Philippi that the only way to have a successful relationship with God is to have the mind of Christ. Paul often reminded the churches that he ministered in that it is easy to have a worldly mind. It is *easy* to be conformed, molded or shaped like the world because we were born in sin by the disobedience of Adam and Eve in the Garden of Eden. That is why Jesus prayed in John 17:15,

> *I pray not that thou shouldest take them out of the world, but that thou shouldest keep them from the evil.*

Jesus knew the higher goal was not to be conformed but to be transformed!

In the scripture text, Paul suggests that we need to think and act like Christ. By doing so, not allow anyone to think of us as equal with Him, but the intent is to mirror Him. Jesus had the very nature of God, but equality with God was never something Jesus boasted about to others. He was equal with God because He was God.

> *In the beginning was the Word, and the Word was with God, and the Word was God. And the Word was made flesh, and dwelt among us, (and we beheld his glory, the glory as of the only begotten of the Father,) full of grace and truth* (John 1:1, 14).

Nevertheless, He did not boast about His deity. In scripture, Jesus always honors the Father above Himself.

> *Then answered Jesus and said unto them, Verily, verily, I say unto you, The Son can do nothing of himself, but what he seeth the Father do: for what things soever he doeth, these also doeth the Son likewise* (John 5:19).

The most important factor in our lives with Christ is our mindset. What have we set our minds to think? What have we set our minds to accomplish? This is so important because our eternity is dependent upon our mindset and how we act as a result of how we think. The Scriptures are replete with warnings for us to control our minds:

For as he thinketh in his heart, so is he (Proverbs 23:7).

For to be carnally minded is death; but to be spiritually minded is life and peace. Because the carnal mind is enmity against God (Romans 8:6-7).

That ye be not soon shaken in mind (2 Thessalonians 2:2).

A double minded man is unstable in all his ways (James 1:8).

For God hath not given us the spirit of fear; but of power, and of love, and of a sound mind (2 Timothy 1:7).

Wherefore gird up the loins of your mind (1 Peter 1:13).

There are four things that encompass the mind of Jesus that I want to share with you. First, in Philippians 2:7, it states,

But made himself of no reputation.

The first thing Jesus did throughout His travels and ministry was try not to make a name for Himself. Jesus did not try to push His way into the "spotlight" at the expense of others. I have met so many people who have pushed their way to be recognized with no regard for who they pushed over, knocked down, or stepped over just so they could get what they wanted. Jesus was Jesus, Lord and King. He did not make any reputation for Himself. He did not pass out any business cards, send out His resume, or promote Himself. He said,

I have come to do the will of my Father (John 5:30).

There are too many people who will miss out on being used by God because they try to promote themselves as if they are so important. The ministry is not all about us. We need to get a dose of reality and realize we are not "all that." With or without us, the word of God will be preached!

Often when Jesus performed miracles, He would say, "Do not tell anybody who I am." Matthew 8:4 states,

And Jesus saith unto him, See thou tell no man; but go thy way, shew thyself to the priest, and offer the gift that Moses commanded, for a testimony unto them.

That does not suit some people because once they help someone or get <u>one thing</u>, they want EVERYBODY to know about it. They are just braggadocios. Oh, do not let anybody get blessed because they prayed for them. They would act as if they gave them the blessing instead of God.

The Bible lets us know that our gifts will make room for us. But our gifts will never make room for us as long as we keep trying to make room for our gifts to be noticed. We do not have to tell anyone that we are a preacher, if that is the case. We do not have to tell anyone we are a Christian, if that is the case. We do not have to go to work with a big cross around our neck, a pulpit size Bible under our arms, and put large Jesus posters all over our offices. All we have to do is "walk-the-walk" and "talk-the- talk."

As Christians, many times we do not have to tell people to stop cursing around us. When they find out we are saved, they will watch us, noticing our language. And if they curse in our presence, they will usually say, "Excuse me." If we do not try to make a reputation for ourselves, God will exalt us.

Jesus was not concerned for people to know His name. I do not care if you do not know my name as long as Jesus knows it, because that tells me my name has been written in the Lamb's book of life. He knows I am His Child! I was telling the men during one of our men's services that there is a man in the neighborhood who has a few problems. I was coming out of the church one day and he saw me and said, "Hi, Alfred." It shocked me! The reason why it shocked me is I am not use to people saying, Alfred. It caught me off guard. Before I could get offended God said to me, "It is your name." Every now and then, the Lord has to remind me my name is not "Bishop" or "Preacher." That is my title and a large part of who I am, but not my name. Likewise, our name is not "Missionary" or "Trustee." We need to act like we have a name—the one our mother and father gave us. Do not be so proud that you forget your name! Too many people have a *title*, but they do not have a *name*.

Reputation is what some say makes the man. It is important, but some have manufactured reputations to exalt themselves, or in contrast, slander us. I have found that people who talk about us negatively either owe us or do not know us. If you are slandering me, but you do not really know me, it does not bother me! Reputation is what people say about us, but CHARACTER is who we are honestly. They might smear our reputations, but they cannot damage our character. Jesus asked His disciples,

> *Whom do men say that I the Son of man am?* (Matthew 16:13).

In other words, what is my reputation? What are they saying about me? The disciples responded,

> *Some say that thou art John the Baptist: some, Elias; and others, Jeremias, or one of the prophets* (Matthew 16:14).

THEY SAY! Jesus said,

> *He saith unto them, But whom say ye that I am? Who do you say that I am* (Matthew 16:15).

In essence He was saying, Okay, enough about my reputation. You all have been with me. Who do you say I am? We may be talked about, criticized, and ridiculed, but I am concerned about what God says about us. What does He say about our character? I am not trying to push my reputation to appease people. I am just trying to push my character, which God recognizes.

The second point is:

He took upon him the form of a servant, and was made in the likeness of men.

No, not "Big Daddy," "Big Momma," or the "Head Honcho," but Jesus took upon Himself the form of a servant! In other words, He was not a servant, BUT He took on the form of a servant. We need to ask ourselves, who are we serving besides ourselves? There are too many of us who like to be served, but the mind of Jesus was that He took on the form of a servant. Yet we will never make good waiters (i.e., servants) because we do not like to wait! The Word of God states,

They that wait upon the Lord shall renew their strength (Isaiah 40:31).

In the context of servant-hood, God is looking for people who will wait on or serve somebody else. Jesus took on the form of a servant, and He did not act like a house slave by doing so. The house slave was the person who had the privileges of staying in the house and not working in the field with the rest of the slaves. To be "in the house" was considered a place of prominence. It is nothing wrong with being elevated to a certain position, but some of the "privileged" have forgotten about the experience of the field slaves. They were not sheltered from the elements or considered "special." Some of us who have received favor to be elevated to certain positions have forgotten what it was like to be "on the outside looking in." But if someone replayed earlier moments in our lives on a big screen TV, they would see we have not always been in "the house." We cannot forget where we came from.

Our primary function in the mind of Christ is to SERVE. I believe Jesus felt like Ezekiel. When Ezekiel was called to ministry, he did not start off preaching, but he sat and ate among the people. He slept where they slept. People do not want our help if they feel like we have not been through anything. People do not want our advice if they feel like we think we are better than they. Most people are thinking that if we are going to help them we should truly know and have felt their pain. We might not be in their predicament now but many of us have "been there and done that." Therefore, we can appreciate where they are coming from because we have already been through similar things. We have the testimony that if Jesus brought me through He can bring you through too. We have to be prepared to serve and meet people at their point of need.

In the capacity of a servant, Jesus even washed the disciples' feet. John 13:5 reads,

After that he poureth water into a bason, and began to wash the disciples' feet, and to wipe them with the towel wherewith he was girded.

Jesus said, *And whosoever will be chief among you, let him be your servant* (Matthew 20:27).

But he that is greatest among you shall be your servant (Matthew 23:11).

Jesus wants to be able to say, *Well done thy good and faithful servant*—not good and faithful preacher, if that is your role. Why? Because you might not preach that well! He will not say well done thy good and faithful deacon, if that is your position in the church. The title does not mean you have grasped what it means to be a servant.

A servant is *one who is dedicated to the service of others*. There are several examples of great leaders in the Bible who, above all else, were looked upon as servants:

Paul, a servant of Jesus Christ (Romans 1:1)

Paul, a servant of God, and an apostle of Jesus Christ (Titus 1:1)

James, a servant of God and of the Lord Jesus Christ (James 1:1)

Simon Peter, a servant and an apostle of Jesus Christ (2 Peter 1:1)

Jude, the servant of Jesus Christ (Jude 1:1)

In those passages, could you substitute your name and say, for example, Rose—a servant of Jesus Christ? For me, if I can help somebody as I pass along, if I can cheer somebody whose traveling wrong, then my living will not be in vain! Let us help somebody through this journey of life. Let us help somebody get up. Let us help somebody overcome obstacles. In order to do so, we have to earnestly receive the job of a servant. Our pride often keeps us from doing so because for many of us "servant-hood" coincides with being submissive. But verse 8 says *he humbled himself.* There is a difference. Submissive denotes weakness, invoking feelings of shame. But, humbled is voluntarily setting aside pride, and there is no shame in that.

The third point is:

He was not a high-minded servant.

The late Eugene Whethers from Galilee Baptist church use to pray, "If I am too high, Lord, bring me down." Some of us do not need to pray, **If** I am too high, but **I am** too high Lord, bring me down! It disturbs me when I see people who have an exalted opinion of themselves. None of us have a right to look down on anyone, because if it were not for the grace of God, we would not be blessed. Every one of us is interrelated with family members who struggle with some of the same problems. It may not be going on in your personal life, but if you search your family tree, somebody was an alcoholic, drug addict, gay, adulteress, fornicator, guilty of embezzlement, or has been in prison. Shake your family tree and see what falls off! Then, act "high-minded." God wants a humbled spirit.

For I say, through the grace given unto me, to every man that is among you, not to think of himself more highly than he ought to think; but to think soberly, according as

God hath dealt to every man the measure of faith (Roman 12:3).

For if a man think himself to be something, when he is nothing, he deceiveth himself (Galatians 6:3).

And whosoever shall exalt himself shall be abased; and he that shall humble himself shall be exalted (Matthew 23:12).

It would be foolish to think otherwise. In Him I live, move and have my being.

In Matthew 18:1-4, the disciples were arguing about who is the greatest in the kingdom. Peter, John, James, and even Thomas with his doubting self wanted to be great. What did Jesus do? The Bible states,

At the same time came the disciples unto Jesus, saying, Who is the greatest in the kingdom of heaven? And Jesus called a little child unto him, and set him in the midst of them, And said, Verily I say unto you, Except ye be converted, and become as little children, ye shall not enter into the kingdom of heaven. Whosoever therefore shall humble himself as this little child, the same is greatest in the kingdom of heaven.

From this analogy it is clear that Jesus is making the comparison of a servant and child based on the child's character. Children are innocent. Their thinking is pure, and their minds have not been tainted with arrogance. Children may get in an argument with each other, but generally if we stay out of the confrontation, ten minutes later we will see them playing together again. Children do not know how to hold on to an offense. Humble yourself. Get off your high horse. Stop thinking you are somebody and learn how to be low at the feet of Jesus! We need to pray for a humble spirit. If we brag too much and leave God out of the picture, we will find that old saying from Job ringing true in our lives, "The Lord gave it, and the Lord will take it away," because we do not have to be blessed. It is not "a given" because of our so-called good behavior or deeds. That is why we cannot be too "high-minded." Who I am, God made me; What I have, God gave me; What I know, God told me; Where I am, God brought me. We need to humble ourselves!

My fourth and final point is in verse 8:

He became obedient unto death, even the death of the cross.

Jesus, unlike King Saul, knew that obedience was better than sacrifice (1 Samuel 15:22). God does not care about how much money we give and how committed we pretend to be in and out of church. He wants us to be obedient to Him, even unto death! Yes, something has to die. The mind of Christ is to let those things in our lives that we hold so dear die. Some of those things are precious to us but abominable to God. Some of us do not have "skeletons in our closet"—we have live bodies! Before we can develop the mind of Christ, we have to let those things that we may love, those things that might feel good to us die. If it is not doing us any good (i.e., bringing forth fruit or giving God glory), we need to speak to those things and say, "ashes to ashes and dust to dust—GOOD-BYE!"

To obey is *to carry out orders, follow instruction, or to comply with a request.* How many have been given orders and instructions? Are there things God told you to do? If we have not followed orders, complied with His request, or abided by His instructions, we are living in disobedience.

Jesus' orders from the Father included death. Somewhere in our orders, there is a death statement. That means there are certain things in our lives that can no longer exist. They must die if we are going to develop the mind of Christ! All of those influences that would stop us from doing what Jesus did and doing what Jesus would do have to die including death on the cross. One songwriter wrote, *Must Jesus bare the cross alone and all the world go free? No! There's a cross for everyone and there's a cross for me.* Matthew 16:24 states,

> *Then Jesus told his disciples, If any man would come after me, let him deny himself and take up his cross and follow me.*

In other words, no cross, no crown.

We use to sing a song long time ago, *If I die now, I won't have to die no more.* If we kill off those negative things in our lives now, we won't have to worry about dying later. In ministry, Jesus went all the way, even unto death on the cross. Because He did not seek a name for Himself, He became a servant and served willingly. He humbled

Himself and was obedient. God highly exalted Him and gave Him a name above every name. At the name of Jesus,

> *Every knee should bow, of things in heaven and things in earth, and things under the earth. Every tongue should confess that Jesus Christ is Lord to the glory of God the Father* (Philippians 2:10-11).

If we let God exalt us, not only will heaven recognize us, as well as our peers, but also the devil will recognize the authority that we have in the name of Jesus. Oh, there is power in that name! Take heed and accept the mind of Christ.

6

What God Wants From Us
Part 1 - Holy and Happy

But godliness with contentment is great gain (I Timothy 6:6).

I beseech you therefore, brethren, by the mercies of God, that ye present your bodies a living sacrifice, holy, acceptable unto God, which is your reasonable service (Romans 12:1).

Happy is that people, that is in such a case: yea, happy is that people, whose God is the LORD (Psalms 144:15).

      Usually when people say they want something from us, we prepare to give something away that earnestly we would rather keep ourselves. We know their intentions are to "take" and not return whatever they have desired from us. But that is not so with God. What He wants from us is for His will to be fulfilled in our lives. I believe Paul gives us insight into God's will for our lives in I Timothy 6:6,

> *But godliness with contentment is great gain.*

Godliness is *our desire to see God's character reproduced in us.* Contentment is *our acceptance of God's will in our lives.* In other words, when we are godly (like God), and content (satisfied) it suggests that whether we win or lose it is all right because we have the capacity not just to survive, but we have the capacity to prevail.

Greed and materialism hinder a godly and contented lifestyle because they block the pure nature of Him. Psalms 84:11 states,

> *For the LORD God is a sun and shield: the LORD will give grace and glory: no good thing will he withhold from them that walk uprightly.*

However, recorded in Matthew 6:33 we have,

> *But seek ye first the kingdom of God, and his righteousness; and all these things shall be added unto you.*

In other words, give God what He wants first, and all these things (material things) shall be added unto you. This verse will come to pass once we adopt four principles for living that God desires for us.

The first desire is **God wants us Holy—**

> *I beseech you therefore, brethren, by the mercies of God, that ye present your bodies a living sacrifice, holy, acceptable unto God, which is your reasonable service* (Romans 12:1).

The second desire is **God wants us Happy—**

Happy is that people, that is in such a case: yea, happy is that people, whose God is the LORD (Psalms 144:15).

The third desire is **God wants us Healthy—**

Beloved, I wish above all things that thou mayest prosper and be in health, even as thy soul prospereth (3 John 2).

The fourth desire is **God wants us Helpful—**

They helped every one his neighbour; and every one said to his brother, Be of good courage (Isaiah 41:6).

Now that we have established the four things God wants from us, let us go through the first two points (Holy and Happy) as part one of our study. A holy God has given us His holy Word. He has prepared for us a holy place and desires a holy nation who will worship Him in the beauty of holiness.

Give unto the LORD the glory due unto his name: bring an offering, and come before him: worship the LORD in the beauty of holiness (I Chronicles 16:29).

Give unto the LORD the glory due unto his name; worship the LORD in the beauty of holiness (Psalms 29:2).

O worship the LORD in the beauty of holiness: fear before him, all the earth (Psalms 96:9).

Commissioned to be the pastor of Greater Mount Calvary Holy Church, it is my responsibility at least once a year to call the church's attention to God's major mandate to their lives, which is for us to be holy. Holiness is not a denomination or organization, but holiness is a lifestyle. Therefore, whether we are Baptist, Methodist, Presbyterian, Pentecostal or whatever our religion persuasion may be, God is holy and He is still calling for a holy people. By holy I do not mean to imply better than anybody else, not self-righteous, not "holier than thou," but holy meaning, *having a standard.* It means there are certain things I do not say or do, places I do not go, things I do not wear because I have separated myself; I have a standard. Call me stuck-up, but I cannot participate in anything that is unholy because of my standard. Thank God for the standard of holiness!

Now, some of us might not be living holy, but we know holiness is still the right way to live. We know holiness is the way to happiness because it gives us peace of mind by relieving the guilt and condemnation sin brings. The devil does not want us to be holy because he knows that if we ever start living holy we will be a reflection of God. Isaiah 35:8 states,

And an highway shall be there, and a way, and it shall be called The way of holiness;

the unclean shall not pass over it; but it shall be for those: the wayfaring men, though fools, shall not err therein.

We should confess that we will live clean not just on Sunday, but from Sunday through Saturday, seven days of the week and twelve months a year. As we do so, we get God's attention. Oh, that really makes the devil mad. But by living holy, we stir-up heaven. We can get what we desire of Him because God honors holiness and cleanliness.

If living holy is restricting, confining, limiting, or binding to us, we have missed its beauty. We must not take the beauty of holiness and make it ugly. We must not smear its beauty with graffiti. We must not deface its beauty with negative connotations. We must make up in our minds that God wants us holy. He is calling us and challenging us to bring back the *beauty of holiness*.

Holiness is still *right* even if everybody around us is living *wrong*. No matter how much we compromise, that does not denote the fact that it is still right to do right! I do not care if we just left the club last night. We still need to understand that holiness is the right way to live.

I accepted the invitation to salvation through a sermon on holiness. I did not receive the saving love of Jesus Christ from a church song and dance. I accepted the call for salvation when somebody got in "my business" and plainly told me I was not living right. I did not get saved until the Word uncovered me, dug up my mess, and showed me the error of my ways! We cannot live for God with a watered down gospel that always talks about "the pie in the sky in the sweet by and by" or "naming it and claiming it." We need the hard core truth of the gospel that bluntly says,

The wages of sin is death, but the gift of God is eternal life (Romans 6:23).

The Word of God commands us to

Follow peace with all men, and holiness, without which no man shall see the Lord.

Matthew 5:8 states,

Blessed are the pure in heart: for they shall see God.

God wants us separated. Yes, we are in the world but not of the world! Colossians 2:21 states,

Touch not; taste not; handle not; [the unclean thing].

God wants us different in a ***special*** way. Our resume should read:

But ye are a chosen generation, a royal priesthood, an holy nation, a peculiar people; that ye should shew forth the praises of him who hath called you out of darkness into his marvelous light (I Peter 2:9).

We are not an "X generation." But, God chose us. We did not choose Him. He looked beyond our faults and mercifully chose us. We are a CHOSEN GENERATION! We are in a ROYAL

PRIESTHOOD, because we have been adopted into the Kingdom of God—the royal family! If the house is not holy, and if the nation is not holy, it does not matter how we fill it up with material possessions. It does not matter how we **support** or **serve and obey** the leadership. God wants a "*holy nation*," and if it is not holy, all our work does not count for anything in the sight of God.

We can also offer excuses for our transgressions, but if a million people do the wrong thing that still does not make it right! If there is nothing ***different*** about us, it is time to re-evaluate ourselves. We are "one of a kind" called to bring glory to God in every circumstance and to turn on the light wherever we go! Not a whoremongering nation, adulteress nation, fornicator nation, sexually perverted nation, a drug or alcohol addicted nation, nor a lying, gossiping, back- backing nation, but He wants a HOLY nation.

Now, a "peculiar" person does not mean we are mystical, weird or acting funny. It means that there are certain things that we will not allow ourselves to be contaminated with as children of God. Call me egotistical, but I cannot get too close to anyone or anything that will contaminate my relationship with God. That would put me in danger of messing up my relationship with Him, and I cannot let that happen. I will not allow anyone to alter my standards. With standards there comes representation. Make no mistake about it. People are watching. Therefore, we are

To show forth His praises (1 Peter 2:9).

Jesus said,

> *By this shall all men know that ye are my*
> *disciples, if ye have love one to another*
> (John 13:35).

We are only able to show forth His praises when we recognize that, *He called us out of darkness.* It was so dark for some of us we could not find our way out, but just like Lazarus who was dead and stinking in the grave, He called our names out and we saw the light. Oh, what a marvelous light! Therefore, we should show forth the praise of Him who called us out. In II Corinthians 6:13-16 it reads,

> *Wherefore come out from among them,*
> *and be ye separate, saith the Lord, and*
> *touch not the unclean thing; and I will*
> *receive you. Be ye not unequally yoked*
> *together with unbelievers: for what*
> *fellowship hath righteousness with*
> *unrighteousness? and what communion*
> *hath light with darkness? And what*
> *concord hath Christ with Belial? or what*
> *part hath he that believeth with an infidel?*
> *And what agreement hath the temple of*
> *God with idols? for ye are the temple of*
> *the living God; as God hath said, I will*
> *dwell in them, and walk in them; and I will*
> *be their God, and they shall be my people.*

God wants us holy and separated, consecrated unto the Him for His service. With all of our imperfections, we are still called to be holy. Even though we sin, the key is to STRIVE to live holy. There is no other defense. If we never make it, the call is still there! If we never rise to the occasion, He has yet called us to be holy. That is why when we mess up we feel so guilty. Those of us who care about the Father's opinion of us cannot wait to get to the altar and say, "Lord have mercy," because that holiness call is on our lives.

When we engage in doing anything contrary to the Word of God, the Spirit of the Lord convicts us. Why? Because we have not been called to sin, but holiness. Thank God the call is on us! Yes, God wants us holy, so He leads us to accept the call. He does not make us, force us, or twist our arms, but He gives us the challenge.

In Romans 12:1-2 the apostle Paul wrote, *I beseech you therefore, brethren, by the mercies of God, that ye present your bodies a living sacrifice, holy, acceptable unto God, which is your reasonable service. And be not conformed to this world: but be ye transformed by the renewing of your mind, that ye may prove what is that good, and acceptable, and perfect, will of God.*

I beseech you means, *he begs you; b*y the mercies of God means, *because he has been a merciful God.* Can you reflect on how merciful God has been to you? Just think about what God has kept and spared you from over the years. The sin that we were involved in should have destroyed us, but thank God for His mercy! Not only has He been merciful when we were out there, but some of us have messed up since we have been saved, and He covered us and kept us until we came to our senses. That is the mercy of God!

Because God has been so merciful to us, He now wants us to *present our bodies a living sacrifice.* Honestly, we have difficulties submitting our flesh. We might as well admit it—we love our bodies. We like the things that will make our bodies look and feel good. However, fleshly desires can impair our judgment, especially when we are young. That is why I work so hard with young people to keep them active in the things of God. The Bible states in Ecclesiastes 12:1,

Remember your creator in the days of your youth.

It is a preventive measure. If we do not instill the principles of living holy from youth, by the time we wise up we will have taken our bodies through so much abuse. Some of us come to God with our old bodies—broke down—after doing everything we can do contrary to godliness. We wobble in the church with arthritis and all kinds of sickness in our bodies. But, God wants us to present our bodies while we are *healthy* and *strong*. He wants us to present our bodies while we can remember one day to the next, operating in our right minds.

God wants us to be holy (i.e., separated and set apart) and then *acceptable unto God*. That is the least we can do. It is "our reasonable service." It is an act of worship to a God who has been so gracious to us in spite of our misdoings. When we look back over our lives, is it really an UNREASONABLE request?

Romans 12:2 states, *Be not conformed.* In other words, do not let the world shape us. They belittle the things that are right and pure and glorify the flesh. The world will try to shape and mold us just like them. Here is how I interpret this verse—I am yours Lord. Everything I have, everything I am, and everything I am not. Try me now a see if I can be completely yours. I surrender all. I turn it loose. I give it up. I know that is when He will bless me. I put myself aside for His glory, then He sanctifies me to become holy. He touched me and anything He touches is holy! When He touched the ground, it became holy (see Exodus 3:5). When He touched the Sabbath, it became holy (see Exodus 20:8). When He touched water, it became holy (see Mark 4:39). When He touched the church, it became holy (see Ephesians 1:4). When God touches a man or woman they become holy. Has a Holy God ever touched you?

God wants His children to be **happy**. There should be no unhappy saints. If anybody has a right to be happy, it should be us. No matter how it looks now, overall our good days out weigh our bad days! Psalm 144:15 states,

Happy is that people, that is in such a case: yea, happy is that people, whose God is the LORD.

Other meanings for the word happy are *merry, glad,* or *joyful.* The people that are described in Psalms 144 are people who are godly and content. The reason why they are happy is they know their God is the Lord! When we know that our God is the Lord of Lords and King of Kings, we should be happy and content because He is the only *true* and *living* God.

We should not walk around looking depressed, pitiful, or sad as if we have been sucking on lemons! Yes, we might have some lemons on our jobs, but learn how to grab them and make some *Lemonade*. Our family members may have thrown us some lemons, but grab them and make some *Lemon Meringue Pie*. If we are holy, we should to be happy, beaming with a smile on our faces. However if you must cry, pick a discrete place to do it. Do not cry in public. Go to your secret closet and cry. Wipe your face, blow your nose, and come out with a happy face! I do not care what you are facing. God is good and He's *good all the time.*

We should be the happiest people in the world, because the Bible admonishes us to serve the Lord with gladness, not sadness or madness. Just think on the goodness of Jesus! I might be a little down right now, but all I have to do is THINK. Not about what is happening right now, but I look back over my life and remember there was a time when I wanted to throw in the towel, but He made me glad! I do not wait until I go to church to be happy, but I have learned to *come* to church happy.

> *Make a joyful noise unto the LORD, all ye lands. Serve the LORD with gladness: come before his presence with singing. Know ye that the LORD he is God: it is he that hath made us, and not we ourselves; we are his people, and the sheep of his pasture. Enter into his gates with*

thanksgiving, and into his courts with praise: be thankful unto him, and bless his name. For the LORD is good; his mercy is everlasting; and his truth endureth to all generations (Psalm 100).

Like David,

I was glad with they said unto me, let us go into the house of the Lord (Psalms 122:1).

I was glad when He woke me up this morning. I was clothed and in my right mind. I was glad I could bathe myself. I was glad I had the activities of my limbs. Oh, *Enter His courts with praise!* Do not look for a happy hour. For everyday with Jesus is sweeter than the day before. Oh happy day!

The Lord also taught me how to watch and fight. He taught me how to watch

when the enemy came upon me to eat up my flesh (Psalms 27:2).

Instead of me stumbling and falling, my enemies fell by the wayside. Then He taught me how to fight! I use to be a coward and every time the enemy would beat me, I would lay down and play dead. God led me to the scripture that states,

No weapon that is formed against me shall prosper (Isaiah 54:17).

Has God taught you how to fight? Now you can say to Satan, "Satan, you are a liar. Get out of my face." That is why the devil does not want us to live holy, because with holiness comes power.

Nehemiah wrote in Nehemiah 8:10,

The joy of the Lord is our strength.

God cannot lie. We are at our strongest when we are filled with joy. Notice, the enemy does not come to antagonize us when we are in revival or in church on Sunday, but when we are away from God's presence he launches an attack. When we are most vulnerable, he'll let something happen to drain our joy. He knows if we will keep our joy, we will keep our strength! God wants us on a "high" that will give us a testimony. Then we can proudly say, *This joy I have the world didn't give it and the world can't take it away.* I can truly say, *If the storm doesn't cease, and the wind keeps blowing, my soul is anchored in the Lord.* That is how I am able to keep a smile on my face. It is written in Proverbs 15:13,

> *A merry heart maketh a cheerful countenance: but by sorrow of the heart the spirit is broken.*

Be HOLY and be HAPPY!

7

What God Wants From Us
Part 2 - Healthy and Helpful

But godliness with contentment is great gain (1 Timothy 6:6).

Beloved, I wish above all things that thou mayest prosper and be in health, even as thy soul prospereth (3 John 1:2).

They helped every one his neighbour; and every one said to his brother, Be of good courage (Isaiah 41:6).

In part one of *"What God Wants From Us,"* we learned that there are four principles that God desires for us – to be **Holy, Happy, Healthy, and Helpful**. In particular we studied what it meant to be Holy and Happy. Now, I want to conclude this message on *"What God Wants From Us"* with the final two principles – **Healthy and Helpful**.

Our foundation text began with I Timothy 6:6,

> *But godliness with contentment is great gain.*

From this scripture, we determined that godliness is our desire to see God's character reproduced in us. A person is godly (like God) and content (satisfied) in Christ. This person is holy and happy. But also in 3 John 1:2 it states,

> *Beloved, I wish above all things that thou mayest prosper and be in health, even as thy soul prospereth.*

I believe this verse is addressed to the saints of God, not sinners. It specifically lets us know that God would have us **prosper** and be in **health.**

For many of us, we have more material things now than we have ever had before. God has richly blessed us. Yet, some of us have allowed the devil to convict us or magnify what we do not have. Although we have achieved a measure of success, we are not grateful. However, there was a time when some of us had one pair of shoes and they were "run over." Truthfully, we have not always dressed the way we dress now in designer labeled clothing. We might be looking good now, but for many of us there was a time when we had one suit or one dress that we wore *every* Sunday to church. We have come a long way! Thank God, He has caused us to prosper.

Yes, God has blessed us materially and not only materially, but our souls have been fed from a wealth of gifted and anointed preachers of the Gospel. There is no deficiency of a Word from the Lord. We are not hurting because we have not heard a Word from the Lord. The Word is RICH. God has made our souls fat.

In times past, I have preached on prosperity—mind, spirit, and soul. But God revealed to me that I have neglected to share on the area of the body. I have not preached enough about the ***physical man***, which is just as important as the spiritual man, because if our physical man is not in good condition we will not enjoy the wellness of a spiritual life. I Corinthians 6:19 poses the question,

> *What? Know ye not that your body is the temple of the Holy Ghost which is in you, which ye have of God, and ye are not your own?*

God wants to receive glory from our bodies. God wants our bodies to belong to Him. If God is alive in us, then we need to ask what kind of body are we presenting to God? The enemy does not want us to talk about the physical man because he comes to *kill, steal, and destroy* (John 10:10). He will do that any way he can. If he cannot get us down spiritually, he will try to attack us physically through our health. The enemy would rather see us "broke down" with illness and sickness because he knows God cannot get glory out of that condition. When we are laid up in bed, we cannot be out witnessing. When our body is racked with pain, we cannot concentrate on giving God praise. When we look like "death's door," the glow of God's anointing cannot shine through. What is the key to a healthy body? Well, preventive healthcare is a huge part of maintaining a healthy body.

KEYS TO A HEALTHY BODY

The enemy deceives us into thinking we do not need physical exams. We know we should have a yearly check-up, but we are scared of what the doctor might say if we go. Even the most "macho" men are scared to go to the doctors, but God has not given us the spirit of fear. Some of us have this mentality that the less I know the better off I am or what I do not know will not hurt me. On the contrary, what you do not <u>know</u> could kill you! We should have a medical exam once a year. We need to see our dentist as well on a regular basis. There are those who will get in a prayer line for a toothache. Well, first make an appointment to see your dentist! God requires us to do what it takes to STAY healthy.

Women, you know how often you need a mammogram. Why wait until something develops before you do it? Men, you know prostate cancer is one of the leading causes of death for us, especially African-American men.

A lot of what ails us is a result of poor eating habits and little-to-no exercise. Poor eating habits lead to obesity. In the spiritual world, we have to have the right food to grow and mature spiritually. The same thing applies with our physical body. We cannot maintain a diet of fast food or junk food and expect to be healthy. If all I gave my congregation was spiritual junk food or fast food (i.e., sermons that will make the church shout) with no substance for direction, I would not be feeding the congregation properly because we cannot exist or survive by just shouting and dancing. We have to get some Word in us that we can feed on when trials come our way!

We have concentrated on the spirit man, but we have forgotten that God wants us to concentrate on the WHOLE MAN. God is concerned with the whole person, from the crown of his (or her) head, to the sole of his feet, right down to the very tips of his fingers. Take a minute and tell the devil, I am taking my health back!

It is not God's will for us to operate in ill health. Black men and women are dying prematurely because of poor health. God does not just want us to live. He wants us to live our lives *abundantly*. God is not pleased with his children dying from cancer, heart disease, strokes, and diabetes, or suffering from obesity and arthritis because of things we eat raising our cholesterol, blood pressure, and sugar levels. God's will is in Psalms 91:16,

With long life will I satisfy him, and shew
him my salvation.

But we must take certain principles to heart to maintain life.

For many of us, exercising is like prayer-- *hard to do and maintain*. Oh, we know in our hearts we want to pray but we say to ourselves, "I am just too tried." That is the same attitude we take when it comes to exercise. Something always takes the place of our prayer time, and it is the trick of the enemy! The enemy knows that if we get a prayer life we won't need to get in a PRAYER LINE. The more prayer we are engaged in, the more equipped we are to fight the enemy. The same goes for exercising! The more exercise we add to our lives, the more equipped we will be to fight off those things that come to attack our immune system. So the question is, when people look at your body do they see God? When people look at you, do they see life, vitality and vigor, or do they see somebody tired and run down, over weight, sluggish? Our bodies are the temples of God. Yet, we can kill ourselves at the dinner table, shoveling the wrong foods down our throats. Some of us do not have to worry about a gun, nuclear warfare, or a car crash killing us. We are killing ourselves with our *knife and fork*.

If we look closely within the African-American community, we are going to more funerals of people who died young due to heart attacks and strokes than those who were shot and killed. In other words, the larger the *waistline* the shorter the *lifeline*. God does not want us to be gluttons. That is why it is good to periodically go on a fast. Jesus fasted. Men and women in the Bible like David, Daniel, and Esther fasted. A fast helps to prepare our bodies for the next level. It not only brings us closer to God, but it helps cleanse us and allows our bodies to rest and heal. It is written in Isaiah 55:2,

> *Hearken diligently to me, and eat what is good.*

Now those of you who spoke cigarettes, drink liquor, or do drugs, this message is not for you. This message is for those whose only vice is that you do not eat right. If you smoke cigarettes, drink liquor, or do drugs you are deliberately killing yourself. Anytime there is an advice from physicians on the back of a pack of cigarettes stating that it could cause **harm to your body** and you still do it, I feel you are crazy to use it. Those of you who drink are damaging your liver and other vital organs in your body. The same goes for drugs. You are damaging your brain cells as you continually use drugs. If this is your case, I am not addressing you. I am directing this message to those of us who are lacks in eating a proper diet, exercising, and receiving physical exams once a year. Our bodies are the temples that the Holy Ghost dwells in and He expects us to maintain them in a certain way. Psalms 139:13 states,

I will praise thee; for I am fearfully and wonderfully made: marvelous are thy works; and that my soul knoweth right well.

In Hosea 4:6 it reads,

My people are destroyed for lack of knowledge.

HEALTH ISSUES AMONG AFRICAN-AMERICANS

The African-American population is only 12 percent of the total population in America. Yet, African-American males have a 50 percent greater chance of having prostate cancer then white males. There are 1-in-3 African-American males that suffer with high blood pressure verses 1-in-6 white males. African-Americans have a 20 times greater chance of kidney failure then white males. Twenty percent of patients on dialysis are African-Americans. Among African-Americans, diabetes is the third leading killer, and it is the sixth leading killer in whites. There are 10 percent of African-Americans who have diabetes that shamefully will not go to the doctor so that it can be confirmed and treated. Once they reach 55 years old that is 25 percent of the population. Thirty percent of all pancreatic cancer patients are African-Americans. There are 40 percent of African-American women with thyroid tumors. It is not just **hereditary**. Much of it is **dietary**. African-American women have a 400 percent greater chance of heart disease than white women. AIDS is the number one killer of males between the ages of 22 and 44, and the number two killer of African-American women. African-Americans purchase 38 percent of the cigarettes in our country. African-Americans purchase 39 percent of the alcohol. Around the corner from our church there are three liquor stores. I am praying everyday that someone will shut them down so we can buy them out. I would rather buy the liquor stores out and let my members put their small businesses there just to get the liquor out of the neighborhood.

Heart disease is the number one killer among African-American women. Obesity is five percent greater among African-Americans than whites, and 10 percent greater among African-American women than white women. There are 75,000 African-Americans that die every year from **manageable** diseases. If they had preventive care and their exams, they probably would not have died.

A PERSCRIPTION FOR HEALTH
The Scriptures reveal that God wants us well:

Then shall thy light break forth as the morning, and thine health shall spring forth speedily: and thy righteousness shall go before thee; the glory of the LORD shall be thy reward (Isaiah 58:8).

For I will restore health unto thee, and I will heal thee of thy wounds, saith the LORD (Jeremiah 30:17).

Confess your faults one to another, and pray one for another, that ye may be healed (James 5:16).

Who his own self bare our sins in his own body on the tree, that we, being dead to sins, should live unto righteousness: by whose stripes ye were healed (1Peter 2:24).

It has been proven that eating right and exercising will add years to our lives. Now you might ask, what shall I do? Well, drink more water. Drinking six to eight glasses of water a day will build up your immune system. Water flushes out any impurities in your body and will help keep your kidneys healthy. We need to stop drinking so much coffee. Caffeine is not good for you. Stop consuming so many sodas. Eat more fruits and vegetables, give up the excessive use of salt, release the grease, cut off the fat, and boil and bake more than fry your food. Take vitamins and exercise regularly and choose life instead of death.

God does not want us holy, happy, and healthy just for us. God has commissioned us to strengthen our brother. When we become ***holy, happy***, and ***healthy***, then we can become ***helpful*** to others.

The fourth desire is ***God wants us to be helpful***. God will deliver us from abusing our bodies so we can guide somebody to his or her deliverance. One song writer wrote: *If I can cheer someone, show someone the way then my living is not in vain.* We should not have a selfish attitude but make an effort to be "our brother's keeper." The Bible lets us know "no man is an island" when God says in Genesis 2:18,

It is not good that the man should be alone.

The Word admonishes us to,

Bear each other burdens, and the strong shall bear the infirmities of the weak (Galatians 6:2; Romans 15:1).

Isaiah 41:6 gives an example,

They helped every one his neighbour; and every one said to his brother, Be of good courage.

Our help is not always in money. We can help someone when we do what we do for him or her, without expecting anything in return. When we do it out of our hearts, we do not have the philosophy that someone owes us something. Some of us may not have any money to help with community or church projects, but just saying, I am with you or you have my prayers, helps! We will never know the effect that words have in a person's life if we do not extend a helping hand. Some have received miraculous breakthroughs from depression just from someone who gave them an encouraging word.

It is not enough for us to talk about being healthy and helpful but action is required as well. For almost three months, after each service, I took an "after offering." The money that was given was raised for the church fitness center. With the offering, I was able to build and give to the church free access to the fitness center with a personal trainer. My church gave enough in the offering to help fund the program for a year. I am proud that it has been such a wonderful success that we intend to keep it. God does not want us to have any excuses.

With other fitness centers, you have to sign a contract and if you break the contract, they will hound and harass you. The fitness center that our church has is <u>contract free</u>. We have several fitness programs for the members to take advantage of daily. My wife, Co-Pastor Susie Owens, and I are in the fitness center two days a week and we are in the programs. Why? I want my members to know that we are in this thing together. I shared this idea with a couple of pastors and they said to me they have never heard of any pastor offering their congregation free service like this program. There is usually some type of monetary fee attached. But I want my congregation *to live and not die*. To those that gave in the offering it was a wise investment.

Whether or not your church offers a program like this or not, make an investment in your health. If we make an effort to do so, God will honor us and help us maintain our health. I can not stress it enough that God desires us to be Holy, Happy, Healthy, and Helpful. Make it a part of your ministry to represent God with your body fit and well.

8

Stop Being Scared: Scarecrows

And I was afraid, and went and hid thy talent in the earth: lo, there thou hast that is thine (Matthew 25:25).

I believe one of the greatest hindrances to our spiritual growth is the spirit of fear. We quote the scripture,

God has not given us the spirit of fear but, of love, power, and of a sound mind (2 Timothy 1:7).

Yet fear often supersedes *love* and *power*. In fact, when Paul wrote this passage he was talking to Timothy, a son in the ministry, whose main characteristic was timidity. He was a person who stayed in the background because he simply did not want to be or was afraid to be in the forefront. But, Paul rebukes this disposition and encourages Timothy and other believers to be bold and courageous.

Fear is *a strong feeling caused by awareness of something real or imagined.* Fear is generated often *by a threat of danger.* Fear is *pain.* Fear is *evil.* Fear leads *to concern, anxiety, and alarm.* More times than not, we are <u>fearful</u> rather than <u>fearless</u>.

It is easy to suggest as one of the literary writers did *"There is nothing to fear but fear itself."* Looking back in our lives, we find we all have something we fear. There are those who have a fear of getting sick, a fear of dying, or a fear of their sinful lifestyle being exposed. Whatever our fear is God wants us to know He did not give us the spirit of fear. It goes against everything He is and everything He wants us to become.

The man in Matthew 25:25 said he was afraid. He was asked why he did not do something with what God gave him, and his response was, *I was afraid and I went and hid thy talent in the earth.* In reading this passage, I relate this man to Believers who must face their fears and often see their fears as scarecrows. This man was afraid, he saw the scarecrows and went to bury his gift (i.e., his anointing, his calling, and his assignment). This message is for those with buried talents, gifts, and hopes. This message is for those who have been intimidated and dominated by "scarecrows."

You might ask, what are scarecrows? Scarecrows are crude figures filled with straw or hay, usually set up in a field to scare birds away from crops, gardens, or harvests. They are set up in the center of what is good with the purpose of provoking fear. A scarecrow is usually a wooden man-like figure with old beaten and torn garments, and a worn hat. His arms are usually outstretched. Often if we catch it at the right time, we will see on each arm some black birds. The black birds are perched on the arms of the scarecrow looking at the harvest that is ripe. We must applaud the black birds because there are other birds on fences, telephone poles, or on the top of trees hungry also but frighten by the scarecrow, but they have the nerve to perch.

Other birds have not recognized that the scarecrow has no power. It *looks* scary, but it has no power. It is placed there to scare the birds away from what is good, the harvest. There have been things set up in our lives that we have allowed to influence us and to have power over us because we have not recognized that they cannot do us any harm unless we let them. It is like a barking dog with no teeth or a howling cat with no claws; it is like a hissing snake with no venom—otherwise threatening but relieved of their power to harm us.

The man in the text was given one talent because that was probably all he could handle. Yet, he did not attempt to use the one he was given. I believe everybody has been given at least *one talent*. If we were given only one thing instead of multiple things, it is because God knew how much we could handle. If He only gave you one thing to do, do not be intimidated by those who have multiple things,

For unto whomsoever much is given, of him shall be much required (Luke 12:48).

Take your one thing and work it! I might not be able to preach like Paul or sing like an angel. I might not dot every "I" and cross every "T", but that one thing he gave me, I am going to *work it*! We might have a lot of things that we "want to do," but we should not do anything that the Father does not want us to do.

This man knew God and he knew what was expected of him. Yet, he took what was given to him and hid it. His reaction makes me wonder, did he really know God? I do not think so. Do we really know God when He speaks and moves? We do not need to try to judge or figure God out. When He calls, all we need to say is, *Have thine own way Lord; any way you bless me I will be satisfied.* This man did not know God because if he knew God, he would have known that *little becomes much when we put it to use,* but he put it in the GROUND. Where have you put the thing God gave you?

Whatever God gave us it is not ours to squander. The anointing, the gifts and talents are not ours to forsake. He gave it to us to see what we would do with it, and I believe God has given us enough for a lifetime! He gave us His promise that He would supply all our needs, but we do not go after what we need because of the scarecrows that hold us back through fear. Some of us are too cowardly to claim our privileges, not recognizing that the scarecrows are just a "front" or an illusion to make us shrink back. We will never hear the Lord say, "Well done thou good and faithful servant" because we allow scarecrows to keep us from being good and faithful in the pursuit of our destiny.

Faithfulness is the key to effective Christian service. Consider Revelation 2:20,

> *Be thou faithful unto death, and I will give thee a crown on life.*

Also, contemplate Ecclesiastes 9:11,

> *The race is not to be swift, nor the battle to the strong, nor bread to the wise, nor riches to the intelligent, nor favor to the men of skill; but time and chance happen to them all.*

We might not be the best or the most popular at what we do, but one thing we should want God to say about us is we are FAITHFUL. Are you faithful, or are you afraid of the scarecrows? Faithful meaning, *dependable and available with what was placed in your hands.*

There are three scarecrows that are set up in our lives to keep us from possessing what we already have in Christ.

The first fear or "scarecrow" is *failure.*

The second fear or "scarecrow" is *our negative view of ourselves (low self-esteem or no esteem).*

The third fear or "scarecrow" is *unfavorable circumstances.*

Wherever there is a scarecrow there is usually something around that is desirable. A scarecrow is never set up in an unprofitable field. A scarecrow is set up in a field that is a conduit to a feast. That means to me wherever I see scarecrows set up in my life, there must be a blessing there as well. We cannot allow the scarecrow to keep us from getting our blessings and breakthroughs in God.

THE SCARECROW OF FAILURE

Many of us will not go forward with using our gifts and talents because we are afraid that we are going to fail. However, failure is one of the keys to success. You might ask, what do you mean? Like that old saying goes, "If at first you do not succeed, try and try again." Have you ever failed but kept on trying and were glad that you did? The scarecrow will tell us that we have failed so we might as well give up! But we need to let that scarecrow know that just because we failed this time does not mean we are going to fail the next time.

Success is risky business. We take a chance on it every time we venture out. Sometimes we have to step out on *nothing*, believing we will land on *something*. We must believe that even in our failures there is success, because in God there is always another chance. If things do not work out, say to yourself, maybe that was not the right time. To relieve the fear, sometimes we have to tell ourselves, I will win a few and lose a few, but with God, *I will win more than lose!* Realistically, we will not succeed or win every time, but when we fall we just have to get back up again! Believe me. The devil wants us to stay down, but we have to determine in our minds that we will get back up again.

One day I asked God, "Why is it that everything we touch does not turn to gold? Why is it that everything we say or prophesy in Your name does not come to pass? After all, we are serving You and striving to stay in Your perfect will." And God said to me, "Failure is the method I use at times to humble you." Can you imagine how you would be if you succeeded in everything? I can imagine people can barely speak and put up with you now! Every now and then, God will allow us to bump our toes, bruise our knees or get a knot on our heads just to let us know we have not "arrived" yet. We are still human even though we sometimes feel we are invincible. Every now and then, God will allow us to experience a little embarrassment or get a little "egg" on our faces. He will bruise our ego to let us know we are not as wonderful as we think. Periodically, God will allow failure, but He makes it so that we are able to get back up and keep going. We may have failed, but we are not destroyed! Therefore, failure should not intimidate us, because if we are afraid to **fall** we will never **stand**!

If the scarecrow could talk, it would suggest to the black bird, "Be careful; you will drop the berries before you get out of the field." But the black bird's attitude is that if I drop the berries, I will come back for more. We should have the same attitude towards the devil. Even if we fail at something, as long as there is life in our bodies, we should accept the gift of God to have another chance and another day to try again. Why? Because we will never know unless we try!

A good illustration of this is found in the second book of Kings. 2 Kings 7: 3, 8 reads,

And there were four leprous men at the entering in of the gate: and they said one to another, why sit we here until we die? When these lepers came to the uttermost

part of the camp, they went into one tent, and did eat and drink.

Their attitude was since we are going to die anyway, let us go into the camp and maybe there will be a chance God will touch and heal us. Likewise, we have to keep on trying even when we fail because failure teaches success.

I went to a funeral for the father of one of my members. He pastored Greater First Baptist Church in Washington D.C. for 50 years. He died at the age of 96 years old. Throughout the program they mentioned his life's motto that was written in his obituary, which was *"I have set the Lord before me, I shall not fail."* His motto is good enough for all of us to adopt. Think about it. If we **set**, which means *to place the Lord before us*, how can you fail? Even when we fail, God does not see it as a failure. We should all adopt that motto. Take a moment and say, "I have set the Lord before me, I shall not fail."

There is one thing worse than a **quitter** and that is one that is afraid to **begin**. Some people are destined to succeed, while other are DETERMINED to succeed. Most people cannot define their destiny, but they know their determination. Even if we have not defined our destiny, at least we can define our determination. My determination is I am not going to stop and I am not going to give up. We should not be afraid of or discouraged by failure. *We can make it if we try*, and that is not just a cliché. There are some things that we did not give up on. As we kept trying, eventually we had it. Are you glad you kept trying?

THE SCARECROW OF HOW WE VIEW OURSELVES

How we see ourselves is important. How do you see yourself? If you do not view yourself positively, do not expect others to view you positively. We should have a good perception of ourselves like that given in Psalms 139:14,

> *I will praise thee; for I am fearfully and wonderfully made: marvelous are thy works; and that my soul knoweth right well.*

God made me, and God does not make junk! There are those who are afraid of the scarecrow because they have a low image of themselves. We need to know we were created in the image and likeness of God. Remember Genesis 1:27,

> *So God created man in his own image, in the image of God created he him; male and female created he them.*

Look in a full-length mirror and find something that you like. Forget about your so-called large nose and big lips. Find glory in your index finger or your baby toe!

It is important how we see ourselves. Do not make the mistakes of the spies in Israel who went out to view Canaan (see Numbers 13:1-33). God told Moses, *The land is yours, and you are well able to possess it.* But Moses—intimidated by the scarecrows—told the spies to go check out the land. When they got over there, all twelve of them saw things differently! Whenever we get a group of people together they will never see things alike. That is why we should not allow people to form an opinion of us before we get an opinion of ourselves. People cannot define me because I know who I am!

There are those who will look at the outward appearance, but they should not "judge a book by its cover."

The twelve spies represented the majority and minority report. Moses asked, *"What did you see?"*

> *And they told him, and said, We came unto the land whither thou sentest us, and surely it floweth with milk and honey; and this is the fruit of it. Nevertheless the people be strong that dwell in the land, and the cities are walled, and very great: and moreover we saw the children of Anak there* (Numbers 13:27-28).

In other words they said that there is trouble over there but the land is good. They ignored what the Lord told them. There were some that objected to what the Lord said.

There will always be someone who will object to our success. There will always be someone who will **disapprove** with what God has already **approved** in our lives. I do not know about you, but I do not need anyone else's approval as long as God approves. They said,

> *And there we saw the giants, the sons of Anak, which come of the giants: and we were in our own sight as grasshoppers, and so we were in their sight* (Numbers 13:33).

If we see ourselves as a grasshopper, we will think of ourselves as a grasshopper—little and weak. But Joshua and Caleb's attitude was,

> *We are well able to overcome it* (Numbers 13:30; 14:6-9).

They recognized the obstacles before them; they were not blind. Yet in the strength of the Lord, they also recognized they had the power to succeed.

We must know who we are in God. We have to get delivered from people's opinion and the way people think. Know that we are sanctified by God, justified by God, the righteousness of God, and the head and not the tail! We do not have to hide our blessing when God has made us a promise or when God has said,

> *No good thing will I withhold from them that walk uprightly* (Psalms 84:11).

Do not be ashamed! I am proud of my blessings. You have no idea how long it took me to get to this place. When I think of the goodness of Jesus and all he has done for me, I am not ashamed. In the words of Bishop T.D. Jakes, "Can you stand to be blessed?" It is not how much we have, but it is what we do with what we have been given.

We may only have a little bit like the man with one talent, but whatever God put in our hands we need to work it! If no one is around to reinforce our self-esteem, we need to look in the mirror and affirm ourselves. Do as David did and encourage yourself! I know with confidence I am the best at what God has blessed me to do. The first song we learned in Sunday school and sang in church was *"Jesus Loves Me."* As long as Jesus loves me and likes me, and I love and like myself, the rest does not matter.

If we are operating under the umbrella of fear, we do not really know the love of God,

> *There is no fear in love; but perfect love casteth out fear: because fear hath torment. He that feareth is not made perfect in love* (1 John 4:18).

God is not a God that will wipe us out every time we do something wrong. God is the God of love, mercy, tenderness, and another chance AND another chance after that.

THE SCARECROW OF UNFAVORABLE CIRCUMSTANCES

Some people think that it is the end of the world when things fall apart, come loose, or unravel in their lives. In everybody's life, some rain must fall. Sometimes when it rains it pours, and when it pours it FLOODS. Nevertheless, we have to make up in our minds "It ain't over until God says it is over." If our steps are ordered of God, our testimony must be, THIS TOO SHALL PASS. Trouble does not come to last, it comes to pass! Whatever you are facing right now, say to yourself with an attitude, "This too cannot last!"

It does not matter how unfavorable the circumstance may be; we should not procrastinate and put off until tomorrow what we are assigned to do today. There is a little poem that goes like this:

You only have a minute, only sixty seconds in it,
forced upon you,
didn't seek it, didn't choose it, can't refuse it,

up to you to use it, you will suffer if you lose it,
you will give an account if you abuse it;
just a tiny little minute but, eternity is in it.

God grant me the serenity to accept the things I
cannot change,
the courage to change the things I can,
and the wisdom to know the difference
between a stumbling block and a stepping-stone.

Come on. Let us pray:

"Father give me the serenity. The peace in my mind
to accept the things I cannot change. Father, give
me courage and the fortitude to change some
things. Take over, or take control, and change what
I cannot. In Jesus name, Amen."

There are some things in life we will never
be able to explain. Some things in life we will never
be able to fix or straighten out. Some places we will
never go. But, our gifts will make room for us. We
cannot climb the ladder of success with our hands in
our pockets! Our circumstances may be
unfavorable, but God will let us take the hard times
and turn them into victorious testimonies.
Remember that an unfavorable circumstance is all
in how we use it. In the midst of sorrow, find joy. In
the midst of confusion, find peace. In the midst of
hatred, grab love.

Do not forget wherever a scarecrow is set-up
it is an indication that something good is there.

People do not set-up scarecrows in deserts or in barren fields. The scarecrow in my life can stay right there because it will remind me that there is something good going on in my life, and when the Lord gets through with me, I shall come forth as pure gold! Do not let the scarecrow of failure, the negative view of yourself (low self-esteem), and unfavorable circumstances intimidate you because the fact that they are there affirms there is something good waiting to bless you!

9

What Have We Learned?

For whatsoever things were written aforetime were written for our learning, that we through patience and comfort of the scriptures might have hope (Romans 15:4).

It has been said, it is not **what we know** but **whom we know**. I have discovered that whom we know can determine "what" we know, especially when we know Christ. Jesus said,

> *Take my yoke upon you, and learn of me* (Matthew 11:29).

To learn is *to grasp, acquire, gain, obtain, knowledge or skill in something by study, instruction or experience*. In learning Him, we will know exactly what we are supposed to know. Yet in contrast, we <u>will not</u> know what we are supposed to know until we <u>learn</u> Him.

Believers are in God's spiritual school. There, we are either learning or not learning. We are either being taught or not. Contrary to popular opinion, the school of God is not the school of "hard knocks." Some people will say serving God is

so hard. But biblically speaking, it is the way of the transgressor or the backslider that is hard (Proverbs 13:15). We are not in the school of hard knocks. We may have some hard times, but God lets us know if we learn Him and study to show ourselves approved (2 Timothy 2:15), we will also learn that we will have improved and advanced to a place that we know more today than we knew yesterday. If our church membership, which gives us access to Bible classes, Sunday school, and weekly sermons by the pastor, has not made us better, there is something wrong with our learning experience. We should not be in the same place year after year, month after month, day after day! We should learn enough of Him to advance to the next level. If we are not learning, we are not growing, maturing, developing or progressing. The failure is not in God. For Jesus said,

> *They which do hunger and thirst after*
> *righteousness: for they shall be filled*
> (Matthew 5:6).

If we want to learn, we have the assurance that through the Word of God we shall be fed.

Learning is an individual activity. All we do in church in the name of "Church" is in vain if we do not learn what God would have us to know. Our present testimony should include that we are better than we were last week or we know more about our Christian walk than we did the day before.

A General Education Diploma (GED) without GOD does not mean anything. A Bachelor of Arts (BA) without being Born Again does not mean anything. A Masters without knowing The

Master is not saying much. A Ph.D. that prevents you from Praying Heaven Down does not mean anything. If Theology is not centered on Knee-ology, then our relationship with God is stagnant.

By now, we should know that God is not pleased with us having an unenthusiastic, pessimistic attitude when it comes to learning the things of God. By now, there should be no hesitation or procrastination when it comes to fulfilling the will of God for our lives. Maybe when some of us were first saved we had an excuse, but by now, the "pacifier" should be out of our mouths and the "diapers" should be off our bottoms. By now, the things that use to mess us up should not affect us anymore. By now, we should have learned to stand on our own two feet! I know some of us have been falling down and getting up over and over again and it is good not to give up, but when are we going to stop FALLING DOWN and GETTING UP over the same thing? We do not need a new teaching or a new teacher! We need to apply what has already been taught and put it into practice.

Why do many of us go to church if we are not learning? For those of us who are "seasoned" Christians, I can see if we were cursing people out a couple of years ago or smoking a few years ago; we did not know any better. BUT, if we are still cursing and smoking, what have we learned?

Some of us have attended funerals of people we knew who died of AIDS, yet some still practice unsafe sex, and for the record, any sex is unsafe outside of marriage. The propaganda used today regarding sex is focused towards our young people. As a result, the devil has infiltrated the minds of many of our young people and convinced them that sensual pleasure supersedes God's desire for us to live holy. What is it going to take for our society to come to its senses? What have we learned?

There is a group in the Bible that is referred to as "silly women" (2 Timothy 3:6). To them I ask, "How many times do you have to be hurt in relationships before you realize maybe the Lord wants your attention instead of wanting you to seek attention from a man?" If you delight yourself in the Lord and stop delighting yourself in men, He will give you the desire of your heart (Psalms 37:4). Sammy, George, and John treated you like a dog, and now here comes Freddie and you still have not learned to look for a *holy* man.

Ladies, I refuse to believe that the problem is that you have not been taught—you know the way. There is no excuse for your foolishness! You should know how to fight those demons in spiritual warfare. You know that,

> *No weapon formed against you shall prosper* (Isaiah 54:17).

Yet, you keep slipping and falling. You have heard the Word but you have not LEARNED it. What have you learned? I have five learning principles I want to present.

The first principle is:

We must be willing to learn.

No one can make us learn. No one can force us to be spiritually fed. As much as our pastors love us, all they can do is spread the table, but they cannot open our mouths and cram it down our throats. We have to want it for ourselves. We must have a will, a desire, and be eager to learn; and it is not that some people cannot learn. They just won't learn!

I taught high school for five years at Cardozo High in Washington, DC. I had students who were smart, but they had no desire. They would come to class late, sleep in class, or hang around with the wrong crowd. They would fail Physical Education (P.E.) because they refused to change their clothes to dress for gym. I am not complaining about failing gym class because they could not play basketball or climb the rope; they received an "F" in P.E. just because they did not want to change their clothes!

Some of us would be surprised at the people in the church who are failing as a Christian, not because they *cannot* learn the ways of Christ -- they are not *willing* to learn. It is not that many of us cannot fast—several of us do not want to fast. It is not that we cannot get up an hour early in the morning to pray—some of us do not want to get up to pray. It is not that we cannot come to church on other days of the week besides Sunday—there is not anything stopping us, we just do not want to come out. Nothing is stopping some of us from getting involved in the church and fellowshipping with the saints. The truth is many of us do not want to get involved. We have to furnish God with a desire. We must be willing to learn. To make a change, we have to be tired of where we are and say, "God I am ready to go all out to fulfill Your will for my life." Are YOU willing to learn?

We cannot close our spiritual eyes and ears and refuse to comprehend, because God wants to take us to the next level. There are people in the church that are satisfied at just being *saved*. Paul wrote in his letter to the people of Rome in Romans 10:9,

> *That if thou shalt confess with thy mouth the Lord Jesus, and shalt believe in thine heart that God hath raised him from the dead, thou shalt be saved,*

but being saved alone should not satisfy us. We might be saved, but we do not have abundant life because a lot of us are complacent instead of extending ourselves to take back everything the devil has stolen from us. Many are not willing to go the extra mile and get out of God everything they can learn and receive. Pick up the Bible. Open and read the Book. Study, absorb, and internalize the Word. Stop blaming others. We have everything to do with whether or not we are learning. For those of us in school, no one is stopping us from getting a 3.0 or 4.0. Those that make the Dean's List, or receive scholarships, or make the Honor Roll go beyond the norm to learn. We may call them "nerds" because they are always in the library and studying, but their diligence pays off for them when grades are given. To achieve that type of success means spending a few extra hours studying; we have to believe we will be rewarded for our efforts.

I also taught at Howard University for five years. Around my third year teaching, the Chairman of the department wanted to talk to me. She said, "I appreciate you being here in the English department. You have developed a reputation of being such a great teacher, but this is not high school. You cannot 'baby' these kids. You give them extra work, meet them early in the morning, stay late in the evening, and you even call their homes to find out why they did not come to class. This is college. We do not do that in college. It is up to the student to set the alarm, get out of bed, and get themselves ready to go to class. The ordinary college professor does not tell you if you miss three classes you can make it up," and she was right. Most college professors feel that they have already earned their degrees so it is up to you to <u>earn</u> your degree. They feel if you want to fool around and waste your money or your parent's money that is your business. Regrettably, some of us in the Body of Christ have developed the same attitude as some of those students. We are lackadaisical—not striving for excellence.

The second principle is:

Even if you do not learn as fast as others do, make sure you learn.

Realistically, some of us may need more time than others to learn different things. In Ecclesiastes 9:11 it states,

I returned, and saw under the sun, that the race is not to the swift, nor the battle to the strong, neither yet bread to the wise, nor yet riches to men of understanding, nor yet favour to men of skill; but time and chance happeneth to them all.

With life lessons, we can be as fast as a rabbit or slow as a turtle. The key point is to make sure we finish the course!

I shared with the men at one of our men's meetings that I was never a straight A student. I did not have the family support or background to produce proper study habits because I did not have someone at home to teach me good study skills. So in high school and college, I usually averaged a B or C, but that never stopped me from trying to make an A. On occasion, I was able to earn an A or B but that happened when I recognized I could not keep up with the rest of the class, so I asked for special help. I found a tutor, especially when it came to math because I got tired of failing math. To help me learn math, I found students who were more advanced and who were teaching or tutoring.

In college, I hated physics, but I knew I had to pass with at least a C in order to get my Bachelors degree. I failed every test. I never got anything higher than a D. I was in my senior year of college and my professor said to me, "You will pass this class if you pass the final exam." I will never forget asking this student teacher if she would help me pass my final exam. She studied with me for two weeks after school. I passed the exam with a C, which meant I passed physics with a C and was able to graduate! I went beyond the norm to learn physics and to make sure I knew it. To some, I was slow—maybe, but SURE. You may be slow but make sure you do not give up! Do not try to compete with anyone or get jealous over anyone that may be faster at learning a subject matter. Let them go ahead; just make sure you finish! Do not worry about who is ahead or those who always seem to finish first. If you have to take your time, that is all right just make sure you learn.

The third learning principle is:

If you have to learn the hard way so be it; just learn.

I know there are many of us who had to learn the hard way in life. Truthfully, it is better that we do not learn the hard way, but some of us cannot learn any other way! Why? We bring things on ourselves because we do not LISTEN. There are people who are stubborn, rebellious, and just plain "hard-headed."

I cannot count the number of people I have told in premarital counseling that they did not belong together. I realize engaged couples do not normally act like married people. They are usually so "in love" everything is wonderful! But, there were those who were arguing with each other <u>before</u> they were married, yet all but swore they loved each other. Against sound, spiritual advice, they still believed their marriage would work out. However as their spiritual leader, I did not see that happening.

So I would always recommend that they give themselves some time in the relationship before proceeding to get married. Nonetheless, they were so much "in love" they could not wait! I have seen some of the biggest weddings at my church, Greater Mount Calvary Holy Church— with doves flying, five musical selections, etc. and not even TWO YEARS later the marriage ends in divorce. They had to learn the hard way!

There are so many things we would not have to go through if we would just LISTEN. I have even heard some people say, "Well, I just have to find out for myself." No, we do not have to find out for ourselves. That is a lie we tell ourselves to justify being disobedient. If we knew how to take advice from someone who has "been there and done that," we would not have to find out the hard way.

Jail has taught some of us. Then again, being incarcerated does not always work with learning our lesson. I know some people who have been incarcerated and leave prison worse. They do more crime when they leave than they did before they went to prison and eventually go right back in jail. Some of us have cried a river of tears at the altar and asked God to set us free, and God did just that only to see us return a few months later, asking for forgiveness for the same mess we were delivered from a while ago. Sickness and disease has taught some of us. The death of a family member or friend has taught some of us. Losing material possessions has taught some of us. Yes, we might learn the hard way, but the point is to just learn!

The fourth principle is:

We cannot get to a place where we cannot be taught.

If we cannot be taught, how can we learn? In the natural, who are the ones that cannot be taught? The brain damaged, the mentally unbalanced, the retarded, those who have learning disabilities that hinder their comprehension. Likewise, spiritually we cannot let the devil mess up our minds and retard our growth in God.

How does he try to mess up our minds? The Word of God states,

No one can serve two masters: for either he will hate the one, and love the other; or else he will hold to the one, and despise the other (Matthew 6:24).

We can get to a place where we cannot be taught and comprehend if we are trying to serve God on Sunday and playing around with the devil on Saturday night! Sooner or later that **instability** will catch up with us. When our spiritual minds become damaged the Bible warns us about the consequences:

And the LORD said, My spirit shall not always strive with man, for that he also is flesh: yet his days shall be an hundred and twenty years. (Genesis 6: 3)

He, that being often reproved hardeneth his neck, shall suddenly be destroyed, and that without remedy. (Proverbs 29:1)

And even as they did not like to retain God in their knowledge, God gave them over to a reprobate mind, to do those things which are not convenient. (Roman 1:28)

There are those who continue to do wrong when they know right from wrong. Yet, there is a principle in the Word of God that lets us know that whatsoever we sow we have to reap (Galatians 6:7). Where there is no conviction, condemnation, or repentance, there is no guilt or remorse and without it we will not strive to change. The Bible exposes this spiritual condition in 1 Timothy 4:2,

Speaking lies in hypocrisy; having their conscience seared with a hot iron.

The fifth principle is:

We cannot let our learning go to our heads.

Although we have learned something, we have not yet "arrived." There is always more to learn, and there is always room for improvement. We might have come a long way, but we still have a long way to go! In Romans 12:3, Apostle Paul addresses the high-minded,

For I say, through the grace given unto me, to every man that is among you, not to think of himself more highly than he ought

> *to think; but to think soberly, according as God hath dealt to every man the measure of faith.*

2 Timothy 3:7 warns of those who are,

> *Ever learning, and never able to come to the knowledge of the truth.*

These types of people refuse to take what they have learned and turn around and give God the glory. I have met some "crazy" people who have a Ph.D. I have met some confused "know-it-alls." There are some "educated" people that refuse to believe we can share anything with them they do not already KNOW. But, we should not learn to look down on other people or think that we are better than somebody else. All study and no application means NOTHING. David wrote in Psalms 119:11-12,

> *Thy word have I hid in mine heart, that I might not sin against thee. Blessed art thou, O LORD: teach me thy statues.*

It is more important to keep the Word in our hearts because if it is in our hearts it cannot get to our heads and cause us to think we are better than anyone else. Matthew 11:25 states,

> *At that time Jesus answered and said, I thank thee, O Father, Lord of heaven and earth, because thou hast hid these things from the wise and prudent, and hast revealed them unto babes.*

The mysteries are not given to the "high-minded," but the mysteries are revealed to the tender hearted in God and He makes us wise. So, we <u>learn</u> to lean on Jesus.

We learn that...

All things work together for the good of those who love the Lord and are called according to His purpose (Roman 8:28).

Blessed are they which are persecuted for righteousness' sake: for theirs is the kingdom of heaven (Matthew 5:10).

The fear of the Lord is the beginning of wisdom (Psalms 111:10).

Fret not thyself because of evildoers or be envious against the workers of iniquity (Psalms 37:1).

Many are the afflictions of the righteous, but the Lord delivers them out of them all (Psalms 34:19).

God will supply our needs according to His riches in glory by Christ Jesus (Philippians 4:19).

The Lord is my light and my salvation whom shall I fear (Psalms 27:1).

Lord is my Shepherd and I shall not want (Psalms 23:1).

In the name of Jesus we have the victory (I Corinthians 15:57).

WHAT HAVE WE LEARNED?

I have learned to trust in Jesus because He is my all and all. I thank God for academics, but it is nothing like my experience in learning God.
For, He is present in so many ways:

In History, He is the *Beginning and the End*.

In Botany, He is the *Tree of Life*.

In Zoology, He is the *Lion of the Tribe of Judah*.

In Astronomy, He is the *Bright and Morning Star*.

In Geology, He is the *Rock of Ages*.

In Geometry, He is the *First and the Last*.

In Archeology, He is the *Stone hewn out of the mountain*.

To the Florist, He is the *Lily of the Valley and the Rose of Sharon*.

To the Jeweler, He is the *Pearl of Great Price*.

To the Baker, he is the *Living Bread*.

To the Banker, He is the *Money to the Treasury*.

To the Farmer, He is the *Lord of the Harvest.*

To the Architect, He is the *Chief Cornerstone.*

To the Carpenter, He is the *Door.*

Oh, Praise the Lord!

I have learned and I am still learning how to live holy. I have learned and I am learning how to live right. I have learned and I am learning if I suffer for His sake, I will have eternal life. If you never learn another thing, LEARN JESUS!

Take my yoke upon you, and learn of me; for I am meek and lowly in heart: and ye shall find rest unto your souls (Matthew 11:29).

10

The End Is Not Yet

And ye shall hear of wars and rumors of wars: see that ye be not troubled: for all these things must come to pass, but the end is not yet (Matthew 24:16).

The week of September 11, 2001, like most people I watched the television each hour to see the shocking, unbelievable, bad news of the terrorist attacks on the Pentagon in Washington, DC and the World Trade Center twin towers in New York City. Questions abound with no real answers as to how this tragedy could happen or why it happened.

Our great country has been traumatized with terror by evil forces determined to destroy our nation by any means necessary. Without any regard for countless numbers of men, women, and children who were not only in those buildings but in the airplanes that crashed into them as well, terrorists viciously took their lives. Looking through our natural eyes, we might conclude that the enemy triumphed and won victoriously.

When we consider thousands of innocent people senselessly lost their lives, it seems normal to ask, how could this happen? In this day and in such a great country, why? In order to find any plausible answers, sometimes we must rely on spiritual insight or discernment. We must realize only God can put something as devastating as this into perspective. With so much happening around us, we find ourselves asking the question, is there a word from the Lord? The answer is always, YES. There is a word from the Lord!

Everything we see and hear today surrounding world events such as this Jesus already prophesied that in the last days these things would be happening. When the disciples asked Jesus what would be a sign of His coming and the end of the world, His reply is recorded in Matthew 4:7-12,

> *For nation shall rise against nation, and kingdom against kingdom: and there shall be famines, and pestilences, and earthquakes, in divers places. All these are the beginning of sorrows. Then shall they deliver you up to be afflicted, and shall kill you: and ye shall be hated of all nations for my name's sake. And then shall many be offended, and shall betray one another, and shall hate one another. And many false prophets shall rise, and shall deceive many. And because iniquity shall abound, the love of many shall wax cold.*

We are still experiencing famine in the world in places such as Ethiopia. Pestilences abound such as HIV/AIDS as well as the drug epidemic that is plaguing our country. Earthquakes such as those that took place in Los Angeles and San Francisco are more frequent. False prophets and antichrist figures such as Jim Jones and David Karesh have appeared on the scene. These conditions are why we believe that what happened on September 11th relates to what Jesus said, *For nation shall rise against nation, and kingdom against kingdom.*

Not only was the attack on America deemed an "Act of War" but also America itself counter attacked Afghanistan, sparking a "War on Terrorism." This generation will be weaker yet wiser because of it, but still the end is not yet.

Cries for vengeance echoed throughout the media, not only from Americans but people from other countries as well. Yet, we must not allow the media or the world to distract us and cause us to loose our focus on WHO is in control. Some have fallen into a state of depression because of what happened to our nation. However, we must rebuke that "spirit of depression" and celebrate the fact that God is still in control! No matter how it looks He is STILL on the throne.

I was so pleased to hear Billy Graham's sermon at a prayer service initiated by the President. I was blessed that in his message he suggested that we might never understand or have answers to the mystery of evil. Even though we might not understand, we do know the father of evil is Satan. We do know that what happened on September 11th was not an act of God. Man being used by Satan orchestrated that travesty. Although we do not understand it, the fact remains God did not do it. We might not like to hear "We may never understand," but it is not for us to <u>always</u>

understand. All we need to know is God is yet sovereign and He is the Ruler of Heaven and Earth. Satan might have "some" power, but God is ALL POWERFUL and ALL MIGHTY. For that reason, there is hope beyond this present darkness.

> *For which cause we faint not; but though our outward man perish, yet the inward man is renewed day by day. For our light affliction, which is but for a moment, worketh for us a far more exceeding and eternal weight of glory; While we look not at the things which are seen, but at the things which are not seen: for the things which are seen are temporal; but the things which are not seen are eternal* (1 Corinthians 4:16-18).

So I propose this question, Whose report do you believe? Jesus said, "The end is not yet." Only the Lord can determine when that will be. He is the only one with the power to "say so." Know the devil's power is limited. He cannot do everything he wants to do. If he could, we would not be here today; we would be destroyed by now because his ultimate goal is to hurt the people of God. Although there are things, we may never understand on "this side," and although there are things that naturally we cannot comprehend, we must learn to,

> *Lean not on our own understanding* (Proverbs 3:5).

We do not walk by what we see or hear; we walk by what we know based upon the Word of God which transcends our finite capabilities. I thank God for CNN, ABC, NBC, CBS, BET, FOX, etc., but there is another report and reporter that I listen to in order to judge world events. His name is Jesus, the Christ. He said,

All these things must come to pass BUT
Let not your heart be troubled, neither let
in be afraid, because the end is not yet.

This occurrence is not the first time our nation has been attacked or frightened. Remember from 1914-1918 our country was plunged into World War I, which resulted in 8.5 million military deaths. Remember from 1937-1945 our country was engaged in World War II, during which most historians agree that the death toll reached close to 50 million people. Remember the year 1929 when the Stock Market crashed, which lead to the Great Depression and 16 million people unemployed. Remember Adolf Hitler and the Holocaust, which resulted in the torture and killing of over 6 million Jews. Remember December 7, 1941 when the Japanese bombed Pearl Harbor in Hawaii. One attack was at 7:55 a.m. and the next attack an hour later and 2,323 United States service men were killed. What about the year 2000 when we were faced with the threat of the "Millennium Bug." Everybody was scared that our computer systems were going to crash and leave us without a means to get food, use utility services, or work. But in every case Jesus said, "THE END IS NOT YET." I am so glad God is still in control! Every step of the way God has seen us through. He has not given us the spirit of fear, but He has given us the spirit of power, love and a sound mind (2 Timothy 1:7).

We must not get distracted, become fearful, or be deceived by what is happening in the world today. There is more going on behind the scenes that God is doing than what is happening around us. He wants us to recognize that *The just shall live by faith* (Romans 1:17) and not by what is HAPPENING.

In addition to not understanding the mystery of evil, Dr. Billy Graham also said in his sermon that this national tragedy has caused our country to unite and appreciate each other like never before. There can be no UNITED States if the people in the states are divided. It is not enough to put "In God We Trust" on our money. We have to mean it in our hearts. Jesus said in 1 John 4:20,

If a man say, I love God, and hateth his brother. He is a liar: for he that loveth not his brother whom he hath seen, how can he love God whom he hath not seen?

During the days and weeks that followed September 11th, I saw on television men and women from different nationalities and religions getting along and working together. But, why did it have to take tragedy for us to come together free of racial bias and prejudice? In Psalms 133:1 it states,

Behold, how good and how pleasant it is for brethren to dwell together in unity!

The attack on our nation has not only shown us that we can come together, but also that life is so short, unpredictable, and uncertain that hating one another is a waste of time and energy. Think about it. Just like those men and women did on September 11th

you could wake-up one morning and die a few hours later. David wrote in Psalms 39:4,

LORD, make me to know mine end, and the measure of my days, what it is: that I may know how frail I am.

My church, Greater Mt. Calvary Holy Church, has members who work in the Pentagon and I thank God that no one in our immediate circle was affected by the horrendous lost of life suffered when one of the hijacked planes crashed into it. I praise God that my members who work in the Pentagon were either on vacation, took leave that week, or worked on the opposite side of the building from where the plane hit.

One of my colleagues in the ministry who is a wonderful man of God was suppose to be celebrating his 25th wedding anniversary the Sunday after September 11th. He and his wife had decided to take leave from work during that week and spend it together. She was an employee at the Pentagon. On Tuesday, September 11th, she told her husband that she wanted to run into the office to pick up a few things and it would only take her 10 minutes to do so. Within those 10 minutes, her life was ended. She had just been moved into the new part of the building, and in what to most of us seemed like a split second, her life was gone.

From this example, it is painfully clear that when we wake up in the morning there is no guarantee we will live to see that day THROUGH. So, we should praise God that He has kept us thus far. He did not have to do it, but He did! That is why it pays to get right with God, stay right, and get along with each other. Should I leave this earth unexpectedly, I do not want to face the judgment of God having departed mad or upset with someone. Life is too short to play around and risk losing our souls because of petty fights and unforgiveness. God expects more from us. We should be spending our time ministering to the lost and showing love rather than bickering amongst ourselves.

Now you might ask, if the end is not yet, when will it be? With turmoil across the land, what is God waiting on? I have three scriptures that I believe will help bring some clarity as to when the end will come.

> *If my people, which are called by my name, shall humble themselves, and pray, and seek my face, and turn from their wicked ways; then will I hear from heaven, and will forgive their sin, and will heal their land* (2 Chronicles 7:14).

From its foundation, the United States wanted to serve God. They wanted to honor God the Father, God the Son, and God the Holy Ghost. Therefore, we became "One Nation Under God." So if you are wondering when this world is going to end, first we must fulfill scripture and humble ourselves. It is not enough to call ourselves Christians, but we must have Christ in our hearts so He can use us to reach the masses. Our nation was founded on Christian principles. Yet, many have forgotten God. They have exalted themselves because of their achievements never acknowledging everything they have achieved was by the grace of God. A humble spirit is a foreign occurrence. Man has stewed in his grandiose opinion of himself because of his economic and academic advancements. Yes, I thank God for knowledge. Nevertheless, we must realize knowledge begins with God! We must surrender all to Jesus Christ. Humble ourselves before Him. Then, God wants us to pray.

Our country was established on the wings of prayer. God bless our President for calling a National Day of Prayer, but in this country we need more than a National Day of Prayer or a time of prayer set aside when we are in trouble. We need to pray PERPETUALLY! We should pray in the morning, noonday, and evening. For those of us who do, do not stop praying. The Word of God admonishes us to pray *without ceasing* (1 Thessalonians 5:17). The Lord is nigh! It is evident in these last days that the only way we as individuals and as a nation are going to survive is by men and women getting on their knees crying out to the Father in prayer. His Word lets us know that His ears are open to the righteous (Psalms 34:15). It is all right to seek the FBI or CIA for warnings of the next possible attack, but there is a God who is greater then either one of those entities. Seek the face of God.

Likewise, seek the men and women of God who are sensitive to the leading and guiding of the Holy Ghost. If we follow biblical history, we would see those in leadership always received instruction from the men and women of God.

King Hezekiah was instructed by the *prophet Isaiah.*

Ahab by the *prophet Elijah.*

King Saul by the *prophet Samuel.*

Barak by *Debra.*

King-in-waiting David by *Nathan.*

Darius by *Daniel,* and

King Herod by *John the Baptist.*

Our country needs to get to a place where we are not just <u>religious</u> but in our hearts we have made a commitment to serve the Lord Jesus Christ and by doing so to daily seek His face. Our ways should be so committed to God that we refuse to do the things we use to do, go to the same places we use to go, or say the things we use to say. By seeking His face, we change our ways because we are no longer operating in "self" but dedicated to serving the Lord in Spirit and in truth. When we seek His face, we find direction, deliverance and peace.

A change will come after we turn from our wicked ways. Then, He will hear from heaven, forgive our sins, and heal our land. How many know we need to be forgiven and our land needs to be healed? So if you ask me, what is God waiting on to create a new heaven and a new earth or when shall the end be? I would reply that He is waiting on 2 Chronicles 7:14 to be fulfilled.

A second key scripture is found in 2 Peter 3:9-11, 15:

> *The Lord is not slack concerning his promise, as some men count slackness; but is long-suffering to us-ward, not willing that any should perish, but that all should come to repentance. But the day of the Lord will come as a thief in the night; in the which the heavens shall pass away with great noise, and the elements shall melt with fervent heat, the earth also and the works that are therein shall be burned up. Seeing then that all these things shall be dissolved what manner of persons ought ye to be in all holy. ... And account that the long suffering of our Lord is salvation; even as our beloved brother Paul also according to wisdom given unto him hath written unto you.*

This is a sobering scripture that some take lightly, but do not think that just because this scripture has not come to pass yet that it is not going to happen. Unlike mankind, God fulfills His promises. This scripture has not happened yet because He is thinking about us! He is long-suffering with us because He does not want us to spend eternity in Hell. God is giving those of us who have not already done so a chance to come to Him. He is waiting on us to repent because He desires that none of us would perish (John 3:15).

The terrorist attack on September 11th "came like a thief in the night" (i.e., unexpectedly) for many of us, especially those who lost their lives.

We ignorantly assume we have all the time in the world to get and do what we want. But, we cannot put confidence in *things.* Our money, cars, houses, clothes, jobs, etc. do not guarantee tomorrow. They are superficial in the grand scheme of things and not worth losing our souls over. Mark 8:36 states,

For what shall it profit a man, if he shall gain the whole world, and lose his soul?

Everything that is material is going to be dissolved one day. God knows some of us are not ready for His return because we are too caught up with our possessions. So, He is long-suffering with us—waiting on some of us to repent and turn to Him. He wants us to receive salvation before He allows the scripture concerning His return to be fulfilled. That is why the end is not yet. He is extending mercy!

The final scripture I want to draw your attention to is found in Matthew 24:13-14,

But he that shall endure unto the end, the same shall be saved. And this gospel of the kingdom shall be preached in all the world for a witness unto all nations; and then shall the end come.

Before the end comes, witnesses for Christ have to rise up like never before. Those of us who confess Jesus Christ as Lord and Savior should be witnessing to someone. We are ambassadors for the Lord (2 Corinthians 5:20) and the uncertainty of the days ahead gives us a platform to point people to Jesus. God said that the end would come when every creature has heard the gospel. He is giving all of us every opportunity to reach out to the lost to spare them a life of eternal damnation before He declares the end. By doing so, no one will be without excuse on the Day of Judgment.

> *If I had not come and spoken unto them, they had not had sin: but now they have no cloak [excuse] for their sin* (John 15:22).

He will be revealed before He returns! Thus, there is much work to do and we cannot let the tragedies of this world hinder us from reaching out to the lost. We cannot let tragedy and disaster bring us to a place that we stop our daily routine or forsake our mission.

There is still hope in the midst of a world plagued by chaos. Even if we do not understand everything, we can stand on His promises. Jesus said,

> *Teaching them to observe all things whatsoever I have commanded you: and, lo, I am with you always, even unto the end of the world. Amen* (Matthew 28:20).

If we want to know when the end will be, we have to look in the Word of God and then prepare to (as the old saints use to say) "run on to see what the end will be." I know we face perilous times ahead, but for those of us redeemed by the Lord, be encouraged because in the end WE WIN!

> *For the Lord himself shall descend from heaven with a shout, with the voice of the archangel, and with the trump of God: and*

the dead in Christ shall rise first: Then we which are alive and remain shall be caught up together with them in the clouds, to meet the Lord in the air: and so shall we ever be with the Lord. Wherefore comfort one another with these words (1 Thessalonians 4:16-18).